12/10

It Happened to Me

Series Editor: Arlene Hirschfelder

Books in the It Happened to Me series are designed for inquisitive teens digging for answers about certain illnesses, social issues, or lifestyle interests. Whether you are deep into your teen years or just entering them, these books are gold mines of up-to-date information, riveting teen views, and great visuals to help you figure out stuff. Besides special boxes highlighting singular facts, each book is enhanced with the latest reading lists, web sites, and an index. Perfect for browsing, there are loads of expert information by acclaimed writers to help parents, guardians, and librarians understand teen illness, tough situations, and lifestyle choices.

1. *Epilepsy: The Ultimate Teen Guide,* by Kathlyn Gay and Sean McGarrahan, 2002.
2. *Stress Relief: The Ultimate Teen Guide,* by Mark Powell, 2002.
3. *Learning Disabilities: The Ultimate Teen Guide,* by Penny Hutchins Paquette and Cheryl Gerson Tuttle, 2003.
4. *Making Sexual Decisions: The Ultimate Teen Guide,* by L. Kris Gowen, 2003.
5. *Asthma: The Ultimate Teen Guide,* by Penny Hutchins Paquette, 2003.
6. *Cultural Diversity—Conflicts and Challenges: The Ultimate Teen Guide,* by Kathlyn Gay, 2003.
7. *Diabetes: The Ultimate Teen Guide,* by Katherine J. Moran, 2004.
8. *When Will I Stop Hurting? Teens, Loss, and Grief: The Ultimate Teen Guide to Dealing with Grief,* by Ed Myers, 2004.
9. *Volunteering: The Ultimate Teen Guide,* by Kathlyn Gay, 2004.
10. *Organ Transplants—A Survival Guide for the Entire Family: The Ultimate Teen Guide,* by Tina P. Schwartz, 2005.

To Luca, Olivia, Francesca, Jason, and Clayton:
May you eat happily, in good health

Contents

Acknowledgments

I would like to thank the following people who helped me gather information for *Food Choices*:

Jennifer Bozek Joyce, Emily Brown, and Jennifer Zeligson of Teaneck High School in New Jersey;

Carey London, Diana Aceti, and others at Ross School, Easthampton, New York;

Lisa Levine-Bernstein, Great Neck, New York, schools;

Marie Glancy and Loretta Chan of Youth Communications, who provided me with valuable student opinions, and to Efrain Reyes, for photographs of student writers;

Karen Braziller and others at Persea Press, publisher of *Starting with I*;

the well-known food writers I relied on most often, namely, Marion Nestle, Michael Pollan, Mark Bittman, and Eric Schlosser;

the owners of three iconic food outlets—Bischoff's of Teaneck, New Jersey, and Loaves and Fishes and Jim Pike's, of Sagaponack, New York;

the personal friends (in alphabetical order), whose leads and encouragement informed this book: Rose Acton, Irma Ball, Eva Barron, Phyllis Cohen, Tom Feigelson, Ilse Girona, Jan Knudsen (my sister), Fran Levine, Elaine Lugovoy, Barbara Novak, Ele Offentier, Liz Schaeffer, and Sue Wiener;

and all the friends, acquaintances, and relatives who listened patiently to my conversations about picky eaters, organic foods, and eating competitions.

Introduction

Aren't there already enough books about food? In the summer of 2009 Amazon books listed more than a half million references to food. More than 100,000 cookbooks were listed, and more than 30,000 books on dieting. But if you searched on Amazon for "teenagers making food choices," you'd come up with a zero.

Until now. In these pages you'll find references to disturbing things—hunger, overeating, food-borne illness—but the main point, besides eating wisely, is to get pleasure out of eating.

Who doesn't enjoy food? Too many people, for different reasons. First, at least 800 million people in the world don't have that luxury. They're busy focusing on finding something, anything, to eat to stay alive.

Second, some privileged people, including a lot of Americans, are losing out on enjoying food because of anxieties. Many, and not just girls, worry unnecessarily about calorie counts. Others are so obsessed with eating what's "right" and avoiding the potentially harmful that, for them, eating is like taking medicine or swimming in shark-infested waters.

And then there are those, often young adults, who are too busy to sit down and eat—maybe even too preoccupied, tired, or lazy to eat standing up. If you're in this category, telling you to slow down, or giving you a nutrition lecture, probably won't work. The hope is that through reading what other teens are saying, you will gradually come to make food choices that bring you pleasure and good health.

"Eat food. Not too much. Mostly plants. Eating a little meat isn't going to kill you, though it might be better approached as a dish than as a main."—Michael Pollan, *In Defense of Food*[1]

"The basic principles of good diets are so simple that I can summarize in just ten words: eat less, move more, eat lots of fruits and vegetables. For additional clarification, a five-word modifier helps: go easy on junk food."—Marion Nestle, *What to Eat*[2]

"Could improved health for people and planet be as simple as eating fewer animals, and less junk food and super-refined carbohydrates? Yes."—Mark Bittman, *Food Matters*[3]

"People should know what lies behind the shiny, happy surface of every fast food transaction. They should know what really lurks between those sesame-seed buns."—Eric Schlosser, *Fast Food Nation*[4]

To put it another way, you have to breathe, right? Would you breathe bad air on purpose? The same goes for eating. You have to eat (over a thousand pounds a year), so why gulp down bad stuff when you could be enjoying good food?

The question is, What *is* good food? The food writers and experts quoted here are in amazing agreement on that subject. Yes, you're going to find fresh, tasty, local, home-cooked food applauded by them and promoted in this book, but that's not the whole story. You'll also find here kindly references to koala bears, to spitting out food you don't like, to the best meal ever, to peanut butter, to tasting grizzly bear, and even to Big Macs.

So read this, eat well, and enjoy what you eat.

NOTES

1. Michael Pollan, *In Defense of Food* (New York: Penguin Press, 2008), 1.

2. Marion Nestle, *What to Eat* (New York: North Point Press, 2006), 8.

3. Mark Bittman, *Food Matters* (New York: Simon & Schuster, 2009), 9.

4. Eric Schlosser, *Fast Food Nation* (New York: HarperCollins, 2005), 10.

So Nice Here at the Top of the Food Chain

Nobody knows as well as most teenagers that eating is one of life's greatest pleasures. And isn't it lucky that something we have to do is potentially so much fun? We *have to* eat. Our bodies require two hundred grams of glucose a day, half of which goes to the brain.[1] If we're deprived of fuel and nutrients, our minds and bodies weaken and we eventually die. So, through millions of years of evolution, humans have learned to hunt, forage, scavenge, cultivate, herd, and change natural substances in order to preserve ourselves.

"HUNGER IS AS BIG AS HISTORY"

Chances are you know of someone who is 100 years or older. Because we take long lives for granted these days, it's hard to imagine the food-related struggles of our long-ago ancestors. If you'd been living in the Stone Age, you'd have had only a fifty-fifty chance of reaching age twenty. Extreme cold, vitamin deficiencies, malnutrition, food poisoning, and other hazards killed off nineteen out of twenty Neanderthals by the time they were forty.[2]

And probably, unlike your ancient ancestors, you haven't been hungry to the point of starvation. Hunger, for most people these days, means that dinner is going to be a little late. It wasn't always that way, though, and, for millions of people around the world today, hunger is still life threatening.

"Hunger is as big as history," says writer Sharman Apt Russell. Back in Italy in 1347, two-thirds of the population starved to death. A potato fungus in Ireland in the late 1800s caused a million people to die, and as recently as the 1950s and early 1960s, the worst known famine of all time resulted in the deaths of more than 30 million people in China.[3]

Only recently we've gotten to the point where everyone *should* have enough to eat. And still, at least 15 percent of people in the world remain hungry. Every 3.6 seconds someone, somewhere, dies of hunger. A 2002 UNICEF report shows that about a third of children in underdeveloped countries are undernourished. Even though we have the know-how to prevent hunger, we haven't yet succeeded in saving everyone. To conquer world hunger we'll have to get better at controlling population growth, preserving the environment, and avoiding wasteful eating habits.[4]

LET'S HAVE DINNER TOGETHER

"Almost every time I hang out with friends, we eat out."

—Shelly, age sixteen

Eating is pleasant and associated with having fun. By the way, pleasure in eating with others isn't a modern, or just a human, conception. Wolves, chimps, and birds eat together. Human hunters and gatherers—searching for edible plants, catching fish, and cooking meat over a common fire—gradually discovered that eating in company was practical and enjoyable.

According to anthropologist E. N. Anderson, "A million years of this [sharing], and we find humans who are self-sacrificing, generous, and fond of starting soup kitchens and food banks. Nowhere are we more prone to give than when there is food to share."[5]

WHAT DO WE EAT?

Steak, fish sticks, veggie burgers—we omnivores (eaters of both animal and vegetable foods) have a lot of food choices these days. Maybe too many. When faced with a long cafeteria line and numerous food options, wouldn't you sometimes rather be a koala bear, who knows that "if it looks and smells and tastes like a eucalyptus leaf, it must be dinner"?[6] Eating decisions can be time-consuming. Should I eat in or out, eat conveniently or healthily, eat expensively or cheaply? On the other hand, the worry-free koala misses out on the pleasure we get from thousands of taste sensations ranging from avocados to ziti.

WHAT'S AN OMNIVORE?

Even though *omni-* means "all," humans can't and don't eat all things. Our long-ago ancestors figured out by trial and error how to avoid indigestible substances and poisons. For instance, the human digestive system, unlike that of the koala, can't handle cellulose such as grass, tree leaves, and wood. So our primitive ancestors, with the help of their senses of taste and smell, passed their learning down to us: Certain substances in nature are indigestible or toxic. Stomachaches hurt. Watch out for that bone. Bitter tastes are a warning, so avoid that bitter mushroom.

EAT A LITTLE DIRT

"Don't put that in your mouth!" How many times were you told that as a kid at the park or the playground? Of course we need to avoid toxic and indigestible substances, but what about a little sand in the salad, a speck of dirt in your mouth? Studies show that "organisms like the millions of bacteria, viruses and especially worms that enter the body along with 'dirt' spur the development of a healthy immune system." Gastroenterologist Dr. Joel V. Weinstock says that successes in cleaning up contaminated water and food have saved a lot of children, but they have also "eliminated exposure to many organisms that are probably good for us. Children raised in an ultraclean environment are not being exposed to organisms that help them develop appropriate immune regulatory circuits."[7]

Our ancestors learned some hard lessons through trial and error, but experimentation also taught them that sweet things

**HOW MANY YEARS HAVE HUMANS
BEEN EATING . . . ?[8]**

Fish	Almost 20,000
Apples	About 10,000
Pork	9,000
Tortillas	8,000
Watermelon	6,000
Garlic	5,000
Pasta	4,000
Pickles	3,000
Modern ice cream	Going on 500
Tear-free onions	Only since 2002

provide energy and salt is necessary for survival. If you have a sweet tooth or love salty pretzels, it's possible to see those preferences as part of your inheritance from ancient ancestors. In short, for thousands of years our sense of taste has served the two functions of saving our lives and giving us enjoyment.

Speaking of saving ourselves, let's fast-forward. These days, our highly developed senses of taste may not be enough to protect us. Can you taste the toxic substance sprayed on that apple? Does the flavor of that chicken tell you it's been injected with antibiotics that may harm you eventually? Our ancient relatives could often blame their food problems on Mother Nature. Our food problems today, however—careless production methods, toxic sprays, and harmful food additives— can mostly be blamed, not on nature, but on human beings.

ANIMAL OR VEGETABLE?

You eat potatoes, they eat rice. Or you eat rice, they eat pasta. There are many group and individual differences in diet.

Around the world, humans have always relied on the same basic food categories—fruits, vegetables, nuts, grains, eggs, dairy, and meat.

Nevertheless, humans are more alike than we are different. Around the world we rely on the same basic categories—fruits, vegetables, nuts, grains, eggs, dairy, and meat. And in spite of the existence of millions of vegetarians in the world, most people follow the path of their meat-eating ancestors.

If you like steaks and burgers, the Peking Man would have approved of you. His diet, about a half million years ago, was 70 percent venison (deer meat). The remaining 30 percent was the meat of other animals such as otter, boar, and rhinoceros.[9] Our monkey and ape ancestors were once thought to be vegetarians, but more recent observations show that they're omnivorous just like us.[10] In some times and places, animals and humans have been vegetarians out of convenience. It was just plain easier to eat plants than to find and capture prey.[11]

WHAT'S COOKING?

Not only are we humans at the top of the food chain (that hierarchy of living things, each of which feeds on the one below), we're also at the end of a long chain of experimenters. For centuries mostly unnamed people have discovered new things to eat and have dreamed up new food-production methods. The most important innovation of all has been *cooking*, that is, using fire to heat food, which humans figured out more than 100,000 years ago. Let's face it, even if you like carrots and appreciate oysters, a raw-food diet would be pretty limiting. As human beings found out all those years ago, many foods are more digestible, taste better, and can be eaten more safely when cooked.

In fact, English writer Samuel Johnson wrote, "My definition of Man is, a 'Cooking Animal.' The beasts have memory, judgement, and all the facilities and passions of our mind, in a certain degree; but no beast is a cook."[12]

Hunting was, and is, hard work. That's why another big breakthrough in food history was the herding and breeding of animals. Foraging for plants in the wild is chancy. Growing trees and plants on farms made life easier. Other major innovations have been learning how to preserve foods to make them last longer; how to mass produce food on mega-farms, factories, and labs; and how to transport foods over many miles.[13]

YOU'RE EATING *THAT*?

If humans have so much in common as eaters, how can we account for huge differences in taste and eating habits in different cultures? Anthropologists, historians, food experts, and others have been trying for centuries to answer that question. In order to figure out why some cultures eat mostly rice while others eat potatoes, why some people love milk and others get stomach pains from it, why some groups refuse to eat cow and others refuse to eat pig—or refuse to eat any meat at all—we have to study geography; climate; biochemistry; social, religious, and political beliefs; and much more. In general, we tend to eat what we eat because it's (1) available; (2) affordable; (3) medically safe; (4) part of our social, cultural, and religious heritage; and finally, in most cases, (5) because we like the way it tastes.

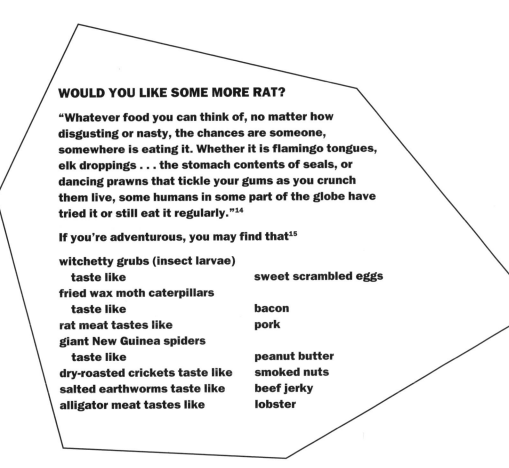

WOULD YOU LIKE SOME MORE RAT?

"Whatever food you can think of, no matter how disgusting or nasty, the chances are someone, somewhere is eating it. Whether it is flamingo tongues, elk droppings . . . the stomach contents of seals, or dancing prawns that tickle your gums as you crunch them live, some humans in some part of the globe have tried it or still eat it regularly."[14]

If you're adventurous, you may find that[15]

witchetty grubs (insect larvae) taste like	sweet scrambled eggs
fried wax moth caterpillars taste like	bacon
rat meat tastes like	pork
giant New Guinea spiders taste like	peanut butter
dry-roasted crickets taste like	smoked nuts
salted earthworms taste like	beef jerky
alligator meat tastes like	lobster

WHAT'LL *YOU* HAVE?

Put aside for the moment generalizations about cultures. Why is it that that you personally love strawberries, let's say, but you hate liver? Individual tastes are often as hard to explain as group eating practices. Even though researchers disagree on many points, they do agree that you're born with some taste preferences, whereas other taste preferences you gain through experience. Professor Tim Spector, who led research involving thousands of pairs of identical twins in England, concluded, "For so long we have assumed that our upbringing and social environment determine what we like to eat. This [his study] has blown that theory out of the water—more often than not, our genetic make-up influences our dietary patterns."[16]

In another twins study in England, Dr. Lucy J. Cooke also found major genetic influence on food preferences and "surprisingly little" influence of shared environment.[17]

We've already mentioned that most humans like sweet tastes, but researchers in a 2008 study at the University of Toronto found that certain people have a special gene that "helps the body handle sugar" so that they "are more likely to crave foods like soda and cake." In this study of more than 800 people, those with the variant gene were found to eat more sugar than did people without the gene.[18]

In a nutshell, even though researchers continue to debate about influences of genes versus environment, most conclude that your parents' efforts to get you to eat your spinach won't necessarily work.

SPICY AND MILD

"My brother likes really spicy food and really salty food, and I absolutely hate that kind of food."

—Katya, age seventeen

Just as your taste for sweets may have a genetic component, your tolerance, or lack of tolerance, for spicy foods is built into your genes. Some people (a greater percentage of women than men) are born with more taste buds. But regardless of number of taste buds, some have a special tolerance for hot spices because they're born taste-blind to the chemical phenylthiocarbamide (PTC/PROP).

ARE YOU A TASTER?

Clayton, age sixteen, explains what it's like to be a taster.

In my biology class my teacher gave each of us a strip of paper covered in the chemical PCP. We were supposed to lick the paper to see if we could taste anything. Some kids who couldn't taste were jealous of those who could, even though being a "taster" isn't that great, since "nontasters" can tolerate all kinds of spicy foods.

For me it was a lose-lose experiment. I *did* taste. The PCP strip tasted bitter and horrible.

8

"Being a taster isn't that great," says Clayton, reacting to a hot pepper.

At the other end of the spectrum are eaters so sensitive to PTC/PROP that a hint of chili pepper on their tongue sends them through the roof. Is the influence of genes so great that you can't alter behavior? No. Anthropologist E. N. Anderson says, *"Genes do not specify final result; they guide development."*[19]

DOES YOUR MOM LIKE GARLIC?

Your genetic makeup was determined when the sperm met the egg. Following that, you began developing taste preferences in your mother's womb. Because a fetus swallows significant amounts of its mother's amniotic fluid and inhales its aroma, the fetus is "exposed to a unique olfactory environment before birth." Studies of rodents show that if pregnant rat mothers are fed garlic, their offspring have a preference for garlic. It hasn't been proven, so far, whether the same is true for humans, but human fetuses respond to a lot of sensory stimuli, and the odor of garlic can be detected in the amniotic fluid of pregnant women. In a study conducted at the Monell Chemical Senses Center in Philadelphia, researcher Julie Mennella found that if moms-to-be drank carrot juice in the last three months of their pregnancies, those babies favored cereal made with carrot juice.[20] So, does that mean you can trace to your mom a love of, or dislike of, a certain flavor? The answer is a strong maybe.

HOW DOES IT TASTE?

What do we mean when we talk about the way food tastes?

Taste, or gustation, refers to "the sensation stimulated in the taste buds when food, drink, or other substances are in contact with them."[21] More than your taste buds are involved though. The taste of clams, corn on the cob, or custard also depends on how those foods smell, look, and feel.

Is it true that your taste buds recognize only four sensations?

No, five. Sweet, salty, sour, and bitter were thought to be the only taste sensations until a fifth, *umani*, was recently added to the list. Umani, or savory, the taste of the flavor enhancer monosodium glutamate, is present in seaweed and Parmesan cheese. Except for the basic five tastes, all other taste sensations come by way of the approximately 350 olfactory receptors in your nose.

Where are these taste buds located, and what are they like?

They're on your tongue and elsewhere in your oral cavity, and they're made up of cells called receptors. Taste buds aren't, by the way, the little knobs you can see on the surface of your tongue. Those are called papillae. The actual taste buds, said to resemble either tiny navel oranges or onions, "cluster together in packs of 2–250 within the papillae."[22] You have almost ten thousand taste buds and each has between fifty and one hundred cells. These receptor cells, which live for only a week or two and then are replaced, tend to specialize in responding to one of the five basic tastes.[23]

How do taste buds work?

When you eat, saliva in your mouth helps break down food. Then the receptor cells in your taste buds, in a complicated way, send messages to your brain.[24]

How alike, or different, are we, in terms of taste?

There's a lot of variation. Females, in general, have more taste buds than males, and when you were a baby you had more taste buds than you have now. Those additional taste buds made you very sensitive to certain foods. Now that you've lost some taste buds, you may be enjoying foods you once rejected as being too strong.[25] Sense of taste usually remains stable in adulthood. Even when you get sick, or grow much older, you're unlikely to lose your sense of taste completely, although sense of smell can be lost. Serious taste impairment, though rare, is obviously unpleasant, because it limits your enjoyment and may affect your nutrition.[26]

Why do some people like highly spiced foods and other don't?

Genetic differences determine how sensitive you are to certain strong tastes. If you were born with a specific gene (TAS2R38 on chromosome 7), you are insensitive to a bitter synthetic compound called PTC/PROP. In that case you're a so-called nontaster—a person who can tolerate hot peppers, coffee, and other spicy and bitter things. If you were born sensitive to PTC, you're a taster or a supertaster. That is, you react more (or *much* more) intensely to substances such as pepper, ginger, and alcohol. The incidence of taste blindness around the world varies. About 30 percent of adult Caucasians in North America are nontasters (tolerant of strong tastes) and 70 percent are tasters (less tolerant).[27] Even supertasters, by the way, can override genetics and learn through experience to like spicy foods.

IS BREAST-FED BEST FED?

You're out of the womb. Now what? Newborn babies in general show a preference, through facial expressions and sucking movements, for sweet tastes. You probably made a face as a baby when offered sour and bitter flavors but made no special fuss over salty tastes. There is a possibility, by the way, that if you experienced salt depletion in the womb you might crave salt later in life. The opposite is also possible: babies who experienced excessive salt in the womb might be sensitive to it later on.[28] Response to salt in babies also appears to be connected to birth weight. Low birth-weight infants accept salt solutions more readily than babies heavier at birth.[29]

Most researchers agree that babies gain physical advantages from being breast-fed, since mother's milk is complete nutritionally and fosters natural immunities. Babies profit psychologically, as well, from the benefit of close contact with the mother. A recently published study shows that prolonged breast-feeding (about six months) was associated with improved scores on intelligence tests given to kids 6 1/2 years old. Teacher ratings of these children were also "consistently higher for those who were breast-fed."[30]

MORE ABOUT GARLIC

A newborn's diet consists of either breast milk or formula. Studies show that breast milk provides babies with the potential for richer and more varied sensory experiences than those of bottle-fed babies. (By the way, breast-fed infants feed longer, suck more, and ingest more when the mother's milk smells like garlic, compared to when this flavor is absent.[31]) Even though it's hard to measure exactly how much a breast-fed baby's taste is influenced by its mother's diet, researchers agree that breastfeeding provides immunological and psychological benefits. And breast-fed babies may also profit from being exposed early to the flavor world of their mothers, families, and cultures.[32]

NEOPHOBIA

What you're fed in early infancy continues to shape your tastes. Flavors you experience in your first two or three months of life may influence your preferences later on.[33] You may have noticed that most humans, especially babies, are cautious about trying new foods. But neophobia, fear of the new, isn't always a bad thing. Your fear of food that smells bad may save you from food poisoning. And if those ancient ancestors hadn't sniffed out food dangers, where would we be today?

Being very wary or not-so-wary of new tastes is another tendency you're born with. Identical twins are much more likely than fraternal twins to share similar fears of new foods.[34] In other words, rejecting unfamiliar foods as a child doesn't mean you're spoiled or stubborn. Parents and other food-givers often jump to conclusions and give up too soon. Even though some people are born more neophobic than others, most can to learn to like new tastes. It's useful to know, if you're an older sibling or mother's helper, that when children are exposed often enough to foods they once rejected, the end result is frequently acceptance, even though it may take eight to ten tries.[35]

In one study of children two-to-six years old, for instance, a certain group of parents was assigned to feed their kids a previously disliked vegetable every day for fourteen days. These children, who were offered but not forced to eat, showed a significant increase in liking for, and consumption of, the vegetable compared to those whose parents made no special attempt.[36]

DO KIDS KNOW WHAT'S GOOD FOR THEM?

Parents or caregivers controlled the amount and variety of food you were offered in your early years. What would have happened if you'd been left to make those choices for yourself? Researcher Clara Davis, who studied infants and toddlers over a period of several months or more, found that when kids were free to select foods they liked and to eat as much as they wanted, they all developed well and had few illnesses. Even if some went on "food jags," eating only one or a few foods at a certain point, they soon went off that food and onto something else. Researchers conclude that children are successful at self-selecting a healthy diet, suggesting that they have a built-in mechanism for knowing what their bodies need.[37]

Does that mean adults should disappear at mealtime? Of course not. Even though researchers believe kids need to assume a lot of responsibility for what, and how much, they eat, they advise parents to set up a pleasant eating environment, provide kids with a choice of healthy foods, and be present during meals to offer emotional support.

SHOULD YOU WORRY IF A CHILD REFUSES TO EAT?

Maybe you've been told you used to spit out broccoli. Or that you went through a stage of eating one thing only. Odd incidents and stages are typical, but ongoing food refusal can occasionally be a serious problem. One to 5 percent of admissions to hospital pediatric wards involve the evaluation and treatment of young kids who are "failing to thrive," that is, who are seriously underweight and/or undernourished.[38] If a child has a physical problem—which is rare—doctors may be able to correct it with medicine or surgery. If the problem can't be attributed to a physical source, specialists recommend strategies for the caregiver to try. Understandably, a child who can't or won't eat over a period of time is a tremendous worry to parents and others.

"NO, NOT THAT! YES, *THAT*!"

As we've already mentioned, repeated exposure to food increases your chances of liking it—unless there are unpleasant consequences. We've almost all had a bad experience that makes us swear off tuna fish, red beets, watermelon—you name it.

"When I was 11, we went out to dinner and my mom said we'd split a hamburger. This was no normal burger. It was huge. After I had a quarter of it, I felt so sick, and now I just don't eat burgers."

—Maura, age thirteen

13

The opposite may also be true. "There's some evidence that foods associated with recovery from illness come to be preferred."[39] Think Mom's (or Dad's) pasta, mashed potatoes, or, of course, chicken soup.

To sum up, human beings eat because we have to and we like to. In general, the well-fed 85 percent in the world have a tendency to ignore the hungry 15 percent. In a later chapter we'll address the problem of world hunger, but for the time being, we'll focus on the privileged 85 percent of humans who have access to sufficient food.

Now let's look next at the stage, when you began feeding yourself and expressing opinions about tastes.

NOTES

1. Sharman Apt Russell, *Hunger: An Unnatural History* (New York: Basic Books, 2005), 26.

2. Reay Tannahill, *Food in History* (New York: Three Rivers Press, 1988), 6.

3. Russell, *Hunger*, 15.

4. E. N. Anderson, *Everyone Eats: Understanding Food and Culture* (New York: New York University Press, 2005), 3.

5. Anderson, *Everyone Eats*, 31.

6. Michael Pollan, *The Omnivore's Dilemma: A Natural History of Four Meals* (New York: Penguin Press, 2006), 3.

7. Jane E. Brody, "Babies Know: A Little Dirt Is Good for You," *New York Times*, January 27, 2009, D7.

8. Lynne Olver, "The Food Timeline," 1999, www.foodtimeline.org (accessed February 16, 2008).

9. Tannahill, *Food in History*, 3–4.

10. Marvin Harris, *Good to Eat: Riddles of Food and Culture* (New York: Simon & Schuster, 1985), 29.

11. Harris, *Good to Eat*, 30.

12. Johnson quoted in Jeremy MacClancy, *Consuming Culture: Why You Eat What You Eat* (New York: Henry Holt, 1992), 16.

13. Felipe Fernandez-Armesto, *Near a Thousand Tables: A History of Food* (New York: Free Press, 2002), xiii.

14. MacClancy, *Consuming Culture*, 1.

15. James Solheim, illustrated by Eric Brace, *It's Disgusting and We Ate It! True Facts from around the World and throughout History* (New York: Simon & Schuster, 1998), 3

16. "Diet Choices 'Written in Genes,'" *BBC News*, October 22, 2007, 1, news.bbc.co.uk/2/hi/health/7057060.stm (accessed October 22, 2007).

17. "Children's Fear of New Foods May Be in Their Genes," Reuters Health, August 21, 2007, 1, www.reuters.com/article/idUSKIM16188320070821 (accessed October 11, 2007).

18. "Craving Sweets? It May Be in Your Genes," *New York Times*, May 20, 2008, F6.

19. Anderson, *Everyone Eats*, 30.

20. Nancy Shute, "Keep the Veggies Coming," *U.S. News & World Report*, December 17, 2007, 68.

21. *Encarta World English Dictionary* (New York: St. Martin's Press, 1999), 1826.

22. Michael Berry, "The Physiology of Taste," 1994, www.sff.net/people/mberry/taste.htm (accessed February 20, 2008).

23. "That's Tasty," Neuroscience for Kids, 1, faculty.washington.edu/chudler/tasty.html (accessed February 20, 2008).

24. "That's Tasty," 1.

25. "Your Sense of Taste," ThinkQuest,library.thinkquest.org/3750/taste/taste.html (accessed February 20, 2008).

26. Beverly J. Cowart, "Taste, Our Body's Gustatory Gatekeeper," The Dana Foundation, April 1, 2005, 6, www.dana.org/printerfriendly.aspx?id=788 (accessed November 15, 2007).

27. "Genetics of Taste," Gene Expression, December 31, 2003, 1, www.gnxp.com/MT2/archives/001553.html (accessed January 7, 2008).

28. Julie A. Menella and Gary K. Beauchamp, "Early Development of Human Flavor Preferences," in *Why We Eat What We Eat: The Psychology of Eating*, ed. Elizabeth D. Capaldi (Washington, DC: American Psychological Association, 2004), 90–93.

29. "Salty Taste Preference Linked to Birth Weight," Bio-Medicine, 1, news.bio-medicine.org/biology-news-3/Salty-taste-preference-linked-to-birth-weight- (accessed March 8, 2008).

30. Nickolas Bakalar, "Breast-Feeding Tied to Intelligence," *New York Times*, May 13, 2008, F6.

31. Menella and Beauchamp, "Early Development of Human Flavor Preferences," 97.

32. Menella and Beauchamp, "Early Development of Human Flavor Preferences," 104–5.

33. Peter Leathwood and Andrea Maier, "Early Influences on Taste Preferences," *Feeding during Late Infancy and Early*

Childhood: Impact on Health, Nestle Nutritional Workshop Pediatric Program 56 (2005), Basel, Switzerland.

34. "Children's Fear of New Foods May Be in Their Genes," 1.

35. Menella and Beauchamp, "Early Development of Human Flavor Preferences," 132.

36. J. Wardle et al., "Increasing Children's Acceptance of Vegetables: A Randomized Trial of Parent-Led Exposure," *Appetite* 40, no. 2 (April 2003): 155–62, PubMed, www.ncbi.nlm.nih.gov/pubmed/12781165 (accessed November 27, 2009).

37. Leann L. Birch and Jennifer A. Fisher, "The Role of Experience in the Development of Children's Eating Behavior," in Capaldi, *Why We Eat What We Eat*, 114.

38. Joel Macht, *Poor Eaters: Helping Children Who Refuse to Eat* (New York: Plenum Press, 1990), vii.

39. Elizabeth Capaldi, "Conditioned Food Preferences," in Capaldi, *Why We Eat What We Eat*, 53.

What Kind of Eater Are You?

A liking of sweet stuff, especially after a meal, may be your heritage from long-ago ancestors. Maybe you also inherited the nontaster gene, so you're tolerant of spicy foods. And if you were a little bit salt-deprived as a fetus, you may be making up for it now by eating salty chips. In other words, human food history, genetics, and biochemistry all shaped you. And those early days of breast milk or formula influenced you, too.

Then your parents and other people started offering you solid food. Chances are you learned in the high chair that you had a certain amount of power. You could smile, swallow, and go for more—or you could spit out your food. Assuming you were healthy and hungry, you probably looked forward to eating. If you had a delicate stomach, or if caregivers made mealtimes stressful, you may have ended up with complicated feelings about food. What other factors and influences made you the kind of eater you are today?

"I sometimes have sugar cravings like any other teenager, but I've learned that eating healthy food makes me feel better."

—Kat, age seventeen

PICKY EATERS

"I have definitely been told by my parents that I was, and still am, a picky eater. And I don't like one kind of food touching other food."

—Anne, age nineteen

"I was a seriously picky eater as a child. I absolutely refused to eat hamburgers, anything with pepper that I could see, onions, green vegetables, yogurt, especially not fruit on the bottom! Red grapes, ketchup, and many more seemingly standard foods."

—Sarah, age sixteen, who's now a vegetarian and loves to bake

We've already mentioned that kids may inherit certain eating tendencies. For instance, Jennifer Useloff, age thirty-six, was once a picky eater and now has a son who eats only bread, cheese, a little fruit, and an occasional chicken nugget. "I do the terrible mommy thing," she says, "and make everyone separate dinners."

IF YOU'RE DEALING WITH A PICKY EATER

1. Offer a range of wholesome foods on a schedule that's reasonably consistent.
2. Don't force food, or threaten, if a child isn't hungry.
3. Exercise portion control. Offer small amounts at first, so kids aren't overwhelmed and food isn't wasted. If a child wants more, offer vegetables or fruits rather than excessive amounts of meat. Strictly limit second helpings. Consider mini-meals.
4. Talk to kids about good eating habits, but remember that role modeling is what really counts.
5. Avoid using high-fat-high-calorie treats as rewards. Kids get a mixed message if they're taught to be wary of these foods and then have them held up as prizes.
6. Avoid taking away sweets as a punishment. The message here is that good kids get good things to eat, but *you're not good!* If a punishment is necessary, it's better to deprive the child of something other than food.[1]
7. Keep snacks small. Limit drinks. Excess juice or milk may curb appetite.
8. Plan ahead. Children who become hungry and cranky end up not eating well.
9. Involve children in deciding what to serve. Kids who help make decisions are more likely to eat what they choose.
   Eliminate "gag foods." On the other hand, don't make special meals for picky eaters.
10. To cover all bases, give kids vitamin supplements.[2]

18

In a study of the eating habits of 5,390 pairs of twins (ages eight to eleven), Dr. Lucy C. Cooke concluded that 78 percent of food neophobia (fear of new foods) seemed to be inherited, and 22 percent seemed to be related to environmental factors.[3] In other words, approximately three out of four picky eaters were born with that tendency, and one out of four was reacting to factors that can probably be changed.

Not that parents or babysitters should give up on picky eaters, as we've already said. If you're in charge of a child on a regular basis, it's a great idea to (1) repeat exposure to new foods every day, (2) introduce new foods along with ones the child likes, (3) offer child-friendly shapes and portions, (4) refrain from forcing foods, and (5) yes, let kids spit out politely, if necessary. Encourage the kid to help you in the kitchen, discourage TV during meals, and try using imaginative names (example: "power peas"). Who would think that renaming them "power peas" would result in kids' eating twice as many?[4]

One last point is that it's not a good idea for parents or babysitters to diet in front of young kids. Preoccupation with weight and eating are likely to make a wrong impression.[5]

WHO'S THE ROLE MODEL?

"My eating habits are nothing like my parents. Actually, for me, it's opposite of what most people might think. My sister and I are the ones in the family who are health freaks. Our parents don't always care what we eat."
—Ashley, age eighteen

Eating behavior may be inherited, but experts aren't minimizing the importance of environment. Parents and other caregivers have affected you in hundreds of ways, so why wouldn't they have influenced your eating? Even if they didn't always get you to swallow your string beans, food-givers were powerful forces when it came to the amount you ate. In most families, at least until the teenage years, parents determine what foods, how much, and how often. And they usually decide on the setting—that is, where, with whom, and in what emotional climate you eat.

Maybe most important of all, those who feed are role models. Studies show that although kids may not have the same exact taste preferences as their parents,[6] they're at greater risk of being obese if their parents are obese. It's too simple to say that parents pass on a "fat gene." More likely, one or both parents has passed on a tendency toward obesity that may or may not result in excess weight, depending on the eating habits of the family.[7]

There's also a "thrifty gene" hypothesis—the idea that people from certain parts of the world evolved a tendency to put on fat more efficiently than others. This was a plus back in prehistoric times but may now encourage diabetes or obesity. According to medical school psychologist Deirdre Barrett, however, even if the thrifty-gene theory holds up, "no trait is ever so genetic as to exclude interaction with the environment."[8] In other words, genes aside, if a child is seriously overweight, perhaps the parents have set an example by consuming too much fattening food.

WHERE'D YOU GET THAT ATTITUDE?

As important as your family is in influencing your eating, several interesting conclusions turn up in the research of Paul Rozin. First, you're more likely to share food preferences with your siblings than with your parents. Second, what you're likely to receive from parents—more often than specific food preferences—is a set of values and attitudes toward food. For instance, if your parents favor whole grains and veggies, you will probably see that as the norm. If they love steak, French fries, and donuts, you're likely to get into that mode. Third, it's widely believed that food preferences and attitudes are formed early in life, but "there is, in fact, virtually no evidence . . . that there is *special* importance to the first 6 years of life."[9] In other words, your childhood food preferences aren't fixed forever. Probably you're already being greatly influenced by friends, by eating experiences outside the home, and by ads for food in the media.

"My eating habits are most definitely similar to those of my parents. In college my mom was a vegetarian for a few months, and for the past eight months I have not eaten meat. I do eat seafood."

—Alicia, age sixteen

20

WHO SAYS YOU CAN'T CHANGE?

In terms of your own eating, you can probably think of foods you used to hate that you now like. Or a food you loved as a little kid that now you can't stand. "When I was a kid I hated mushrooms, onions, tomatoes, mayo, green olives, cabbage, stinky/bleu cheeses, but I grew to like them," says "kloomis" on the website Chowhound, where people who claim that they "live to eat" share comments on taste preferences.[10] Possible explanations for reversing your tastes as you get older are (1) physical changes in your body, (2) new associations and food memories that take the place of old ones, and (3) the urge to be independent and to differentiate yourself.

The urge to be independent, sometimes known as teenage rebellion, often shows up in food-related situations. As anthropologist Leon Rappoport says, "One of the unmistakable and often unconscious tactics of teenagers in Western society who are trying to establish a sense of identity apart from their parents frequently is played out at the dinner table when they begin to reject or criticize familiar family food items."[11]

WHAT DOES YOUR FAMILY EAT?

Put aside taste preferences for the moment. Several other factors affect your family's diet. Most of us, except for billionaires with private planes and chefs, are restricted in our eating by cost and availability. We'll talk later about eating at home versus eating out and food costs. For the moment we're assuming you aren't a billionaire and you aren't starving. Other factors that may influence your family's diet are safety and snobbery. That is, whoever buys your food may avoid an item thought to be risky (raw spinach, because of bacteria, or certain fish, because of mercury level) or may choose an item thought to be "in" (cake from a noted bakery or, let's say, pomegranate juice).

21

What your family consumes, then, depends on several factors, but in general, when you eat at home, what type of food is usually served? Paul Rozin says, "Suppose one wishes to know as much as possible about the foods another person likes and eats and can ask that person only one question. . . . There is no doubt about it, the question should be, What is your culture or ethnic group?"[12]

In the United States many people can't answer the question What am I? so easily. Cultures blend, and in a melting-pot nation we all experience new things, edible and otherwise. An African immigrant may learn to prefer sliced white bread. An Italian American may hate pizza. Our population is so diverse and our range of cuisines so wide that the description *English*, or *German*, or *African* American may not give Rozin, or anybody, enough to go on in predicting food tastes. Nevertheless, we still do tend to include, or even favor, the food of our origins, and many of us cling forever to family habits and recipes.

"WE ARE WHERE WE EAT"

How have these ethnic differences in food come about? Geography is crucial. Over the centuries, in different parts of the world, certain grains and plants have grown better than others and certain animals thrived. Quality of the soil, climate, and weather have affected food production. Forested areas yield animals, nuts, and certain fruits. People who live near water have relied on fish and seafood. Population density has often affected what, and how much, people eat. For instance, if a particular culture consumes a lot of meat, chances are the population density is low.[13] Think about cattle ranches—lots of land and few people. In the past, human diets were determined by location, location, location. Even today some food writers think that the phrase "we *are* what we eat" isn't as true as "we are *where* we eat."[14]

IS PASTA ITALIAN?

Even though it's possible these days to mix and match cuisines, why do many families, when they eat at home, stay within a certain range? At your house, let's say, meat and potatoes are typical, whereas at your friend's house the basics are mostly vegetables and rice. Each family may be following an eating pattern passed down from previous generations, a diet that's a combination of convenience, habit, nostalgia, comfort level, and taste preference. The stories of how different cuisines evolved go back to the Pleistocene Age, when ecological shifts affected plant growth. In some regions rice became the preferred staple, in other regions potatoes or corn.

Where it was possible to raise animals, particular animals came to be preferred. If a favorite meal in your house is lamb, lentils, and hummus, it may be that you can trace your roots back to the Near East, where, beginning around 9000 BC, wheat and barley were first cultivated and sheep, goats, and chickpeas were eaten.[15] Or maybe you barely know where the Near East is, and you think of a lamb dinner as something that comes from a recipe in a food magazine.

At the same time that wheat and barley flourished in the Near East, staples of rice, millet, and soybeans grew well in China and other Asian countries. Pigs, chicken, and various vegetables were sources of protein in Asia. Africa developed distinct grains and tuber crops, particularly large sweet potatoes. In Mexico millet came first but maize, or corn, eventually grew better. Beans and fish were staples, and vitamin-rich crops included tomatoes, chiles, squash, and avocados. Those same vegetables, plus peanuts and potatoes, did well in South America.[16]

You get the idea. Everybody's family came from someplace. In the past, food production was local, but even now that it's global, many families still stick to old preferences. Along the way, certain regions and countries developed individual styles of food preparation (cuisines), but there has been so much overlap and exchange of foods that historians warn us not to oversimplify.

If we talk about "French food," "Italian food," or "American food," we may be conveying something in general about ingredients, cooking methods, and flavors, but "ethnic food" is hard to define. "It changes constantly with shifting patterns of politics, conquest, and trade." Pasta is Italian, right? Well, the early Romans had none,[17] but the Chinese ate something similar as early as 4000 BC And what is "Spanish food"? Are we talking about food from Spain, Mexico, Peru, or Brazil?

WE ARE *WHERE* WE EAT

Loretta Chan, age twenty, grew up in New York and was closely involved with her father's restaurant. (Her job as a kid was to count out fortune cookies and staple them into little bags). On a night off, her father lovingly prepared an elaborate Chinese meal of steamed sea bass, bird's nest soup, and cellophane noodles for her and her younger sister and brother. Loretta's siblings ate without comment in front of the TV set.

But on his next night off, when Loretta's father cooked steak, baked potatoes, and corn, her brother and sister were thrilled. "Wow," they said, "just like at Georgia Diner!"[18]

BUTTER AND OLIVE OIL

Nevertheless, it's useful to be able to describe a cuisine, or a restaurant, as Indian, Japanese, or American. Often, in addition to certain predictable ingredients, a cuisine is defined by the type of fat used for cooking and flavoring. Olive oil, plentiful in southern Europe, became the fat of choice in Italy and Greece. In northern Europe, where there was more livestock, animal fats were used. Butter, for instance, is important in classic French cooking. Another major difference among cuisines is in choices of herbs and spices. One cuisine may favor ginger and cinnamon, another basil and oregano.

As we said before, parents and relatives are usually food role models. If they learned from their parents and grandparents to appreciate corned beef, or smoked salmon, or black-eyed peas, there's a good chance that we, too, will be drawn to those edibles. Family food loyalties, by the way, often last across the years and across the miles. "It is a common feature of migration that 'ethnic' cuisine is retained as far as possible after migration, but some ingredients may have to be changed."[19]

Unfortunately, a downside of favoring your own way of eating is that food preferences sometimes become food prejudices. "'Ours' is right and superior and smells good; 'theirs' is wrong and inferior and smells bad, no matter who 'they' are," says food anthropologist Leon Rappoport. This silly sense of superiority crops up in ethnic slurs. (Germans are "krauts," Mexicans are "beaners.") A certain encyclopedia of ethnic humor contains a whole chapter of insults based on ethnic food stereotypes.[20]

NO MILK, PLEASE

Still other factors may affect your style of eating. Particular foods may be rejected by you and your family for medical reasons. For instance, many people around the world experience discomfort when they consume milk. (We're speaking here of milk from animals, of course, as opposed to substitutes derived from soy or rice.) Even though newborn babies of all ethnicities produce lactase, an enzyme that allows them to digest milk, that ability doesn't necessarily last.

"Ninety-six per cent of people who come from West European stock continue to produce the enzyme throughout life and are therefore able to drink fresh milk without discomfort. But 75 per cent of Africans, Indians, Persians, Arabs, and East Europeans stop producing lactase in early maturity and therefore suffer nausea, flatulence, abdominal pain or diarrhoea when they drink more than the smallest quantity." There is disagreement about why some groups are milk intolerant, but the explanation probably has to do with differences in climate and exposure to sunlight among various peoples.[21]

KILLING THE FATTED CALF

Does your family look forward to special foods on religious holidays? Or maybe, for religious reasons, there are certain foods you and your family never eat. Part of the explanation of religious dietary laws has to do with practicalities in ancient times ("Pork can be a dangerous meat in a hot climate"). Another part may be the need of groups to define themselves and create a sense of unity through dietary rules.[22]

In addition to specific prohibitions (Jews and Muslims traditionally don't eat pork, many Buddhists are vegetarians), religious groups may encourage fasting and/or discourage gluttony. "Judaism, Christianity, Islam, Hinduism, and Buddhism warn against overindulgence in hedonistic pleasures of the flesh. Instead they emphasize moral ideals of virtue based on restrictive diets or abstinence."[23] Among Quakers, the Amish, and certain other Christian sects, plainness in eating, as in all things, is the ideal. Although wine is used in religious rituals of some Christians (Roman Catholics, Eastern Orthodox Christians, and certain Protestant denominations), Mormons, for instance, "specifically forbid wine or any alcoholic drinks because of their stimulant properties."[24]

Religious dietary guidelines are intended to (1) help people communicate with God, by offering thanks; (2) show their faith, by accepting divine directives; and (3) develop discipline, through fasting.

FACING A DIETARY-RULES TEST

If you and your family observe religious dietary rules, there may come a day when you personally are tested. For anthropologist Leon Rappoport, the "frightening enigma" was his experience as a twelve-year-old. In his home no pork was eaten, in keeping with Jewish dietary laws, but as a Boy Scout he found himself tasting "ham and bacon, half expecting to be struck down by an Orthodox Jewish thunderbolt, or at least a major stomach ache." Rappoport concludes that he "got away clean and went on to become a typically omnivorous teenager, primarily concerned with quantity, not quality."[25]

Other teenagers, of course, continue to observe religious dietary laws regardless of temptations and complications. These days, certain schools and organizations are working at getting a diverse group of kids together without asking them to sacrifice their own group identities. For instance, Camp IF (Interfaith Action) sponsored by the New England branch

HOW DOES RELIGION AFFECT DIET?[26]

What does kosher *mean*?

Kosher is the English form of a Hebrew word referring to the ancient Jewish laws of *Kashrut. Kosher* means "proper, fit for ritual use." These laws establish the correct way to process and prepare certain foods, and they rule out such foods as pork, shellfish, and meat eaten at the same time as dairy products. Not all Jews today adhere to these laws, and some "keep kosher" only at home.

What is Ramadan?

In the Muslim faith (Islam), Ramadan is the ninth month of the Islamic year, to be devoted to praying, fasting, and performing acts of charity. Most Muslims are required to refrain from food and drink during daylight hours for the entire month. The fast is broken each evening by a meal that traditionally includes dates and sweet drinks. Ramadan is meant to remind Muslims of the poor, to cleanse the body, and to foster serenity and spiritual devotion.

In what religion is the cow sacred?

Many Hindus are strict vegetarians. Those who do eat meat are forbidden to eat beef because cows occupy a sacred place in their religion. Products from the cow, such as milk and yogurt, which *are* permitted, are thought to promote purity of mind and body. The eating of pork, ducks, and certain shellfish is also avoided. Devout Hindus fast on Sundays, on the eighteen major holidays, and on birthdays and anniversaries.

In what religion is it considered wrong to kill even a mosquito?

Jainism, one of the oldest religions in India, has many strict food prohibitions. Because the Jains believe we are going to be reborn in a different form, they deeply respect all animal life. Other guidelines of Jainism include the following:[27]

1. Do not eat meat of any kind. Establish asylums for old and diseased animals. Leave out food for rats if need be.
2. Filter water to save the microscopic organisms you would otherwise swallow.
3. Do not drink water after dark—you might swallow a small insect by mistake.
4. Do not eat seeded food such as tomatoes and figs because each seed is alive.
5. Fast often. Fasts may last from twenty-four hours to two years.

What dietary practices are observed in Christianity?

In general, food prohibitions are few in Christianity. An exception is the Protestant sect Seventh-day Adventists, who may be vegetarians. (They avoid tea, coffee, and alcohol as well as meat.) Roman Catholics, until 1966 when the ruling changed, were not permitted to eat meat on Fridays.

Christians emphasize moderation and, in some denominations, fasting, especially during Lent (the forty days before Easter). Unleavened bread and wine (sometimes grape juice) have a special significance in the rite of communion.

Alicia Ball enjoys a taste of challah (yeasty, braided egg bread) at her family's Sabbath dinner.

of the Anti-Defamation League, brings together eighty teens of different faiths—Muslim, Jewish, and Christian—for the usual camp activities, plus discussions about similarities and differences among their groups. A kosher kitchen for Jewish participants and a halal one for Muslims provide comfort for those campers and foster cross-cultural understanding.[28]

MRS. GREEN SAYS . . .

We've already established that eating habits are influenced by family background. But besides family, most of us are also influenced by popular beliefs, expectations, and judgments in our society at large. Eating is a social activity. We share meals with others both inside and outside our homes. We see what other people are eating, and we compare ourselves to them. Maybe you came home from school with advice from a teacher. "Mrs. Green says brown rice is healthier than white rice!" "Mr. Johnson says blueberries improve your memory!" On the other hand, maybe you can relate to Katya and Caroline, who say that school has had little impact on their eating habits.

"School has had no effect on my attitude toward eating or my knowledge of a healthy diet."
—Katya, age seventeen

"I remember learning about healthy eating a lot in school, but like most things in school, I didn't really care."
—Caroline, age seventeen

Books, newspapers, and Internet websites give us the latest on what is supposedly healthy or unhealthy, desirable or undesirable. And we haven't even mentioned yet the enormous influence of commercial messages for food products.

ME STEAK, YOU SALAD!

Because eating is social and foods are often symbolic, as we get older some of us make eating choices in order to try to project a particular self-image. For instance, choices may be based on our idea of what is masculine or feminine.

"I think most girls are worried about what others think about their food choices. They try to eat less to look cool, ordering salads, whereas boys eat what they want and don't care how messy the food is, or how much they eat of it."
—Kimmy, age seventeen

According to Leon Rappoport, "Marketing studies conducted in the 1950s and '60s by the psychoanalyst Ernst Dichter showed that meat, potatoes, and coffee were considered strongly masculine by consumers, whereas rice, cake, and tea were seen as feminine. . . . Most 'light' foods—salads, yogurt, fruit—have a feminine image, while heavy, smelly foods—herring, pot roast, corned beef and cabbage—are seen as masculine. . . . Some foods, however, such as chicken and oranges, were found by Dichter to be 'bisexual' or gender neutral."[29]

Ask yourself whether those old food associations still exist or whether we've become less sexist today in our attitudes toward food.

"I don't really think there is a huge difference between boys' and girls' eating. Girls might be a little more conscious of how much they're eating and the calorie count."
—Katya, age seventeen

E. N. Anderson would probably say that food sexism still exists. He describes a common experiment done by anthropology students. A male and a female student go into a restaurant together. The woman orders a steak and the man orders fish. If the students are drinking age, the woman orders whiskey and the man, white wine. According to Anderson, waiters almost always reverse the order when they serve.[30]

BIG MAC OR FILET MIGNON?

Another interest of anthropologists is the notion that people develop food preferences by following the lead of persons they admire or identify with. Leon Rappoport claims that the urge can be "traced back to our hunter ancestors, who apparently admired powerful animals and believed that they would gain some of that strength by eating . . . the heart of the lion, perhaps."[31]

A present-day version of that impulse, he says, is found when people, trying to move up in social class or prestige, give up their former way of eating and start to go upscale, in imitation of those they admire.

YOU'RE WEIRD!

Do you judge people on the basis of what they eat? For the moment we're not talking about quantity but about specific

If you're a burger-and-fries person, this gecko-on-a-skewer would probably be a big leap.

foods. Have you been on either the giving or the receiving end of jokes about granola eaters, or kids who are human garbage pails, or kids who smell of garlic or some other flavoring? Katya remembers being teased about a really healthy snack she took to school, but the kids she hangs out with now, she says, "never make fun of someone for what they're eating."

Whether we like it or not, people judge each other, so it figures that eating style may be one of the criteria. Table manners, of course, are often a basis for criticism, not only from parents toward kids but also from kids toward each other. But table manners aside, are you ever turned off by the look or smell of food that other kids eat? If so, ask yourself what your judgment is based on. Is it a matter of thinking, *You're weird because you don't eat the way I do?*

FRUIT-FILLED COOKIES OR CHOCOLATE CHIP?

How much do you think strangers can tell about you by knowing your eating habits? It's a given that advertisers want to know your tastes so they can try to sell more stuff to you. But political strategists—people who conduct election polls—who would expect *them* to care about food preferences? And yet once you reach voting age, they may care. "Although gender, religion, and other basic personal data are much more valuable for pollsters, information about eating—along with travel and hobbies—are in the second tier of data used to predict how someone might vote," says Christopher Mann of MSHC Partners, a communications firm that helps candidates get out their messages.[32]

In other words, MSHC Partners, on the basis of people's eating preferences, claims to be able to predict how they're likely to vote. Dr. Pepper is supposedly a "Republican soda," while Pepsi and Sprite are "Democratic." According to political commentator Matthew Dowd, Republicans tend to prefer different store-bought cookies and fast-food restaurants from those chosen by Democrats, and "anything organic or more Whole Foods-y skews more Democratic."[33] As you can imagine, many are skeptical of this kind of information. CNN strategist James Carville says, "Suppose I found out people who drink cappuccinos are Democrats and black coffee drinkers are likely to vote Republican? So what? All kinds of other things are more predictive and less expensive to find out."[34]

AND THE BIGGEST INFLUENCE OF ALL

"When I was eight, I saw a commercial for Skippy Squeeze Stixs, with a song that was really catchy and an animated character on a skateboard. To this day I still sing the tune. I never actually cared that much for the Stixs, but I kept eating them because I liked the commercial."

—Ashley, age sixteen

Do you admit to making food choices based on ads you've seen and heard? In spite of genetics, biochemistry, geography, and ethnicity, the influence on your eating that may be greatest is television. Food advertisements come at you, of course, from newspapers, magazines, radio, signs and billboards, and other places, but television is thought to be the most powerful source. A 2007 study reports that thirteen- to seventeen-year-olds watch an average of 17 food ads a day, or more than 6,000 a year. That adds up to almost forty-one hours.[35]

"That might not be a problem," says journalist Sally Squires, "if the ads promoted nutritious fare, such as fruit, vegetables, whole grains and low-fat dairy products. But the report . . . highlights how TV commercials tout mostly junk food. Candy and snacks accounted for a third of the food commercials, while 28 percent were for cereals, many of them loaded with added sugar, and 10 percent were for fast food."[36]

Commercials encourage kids to eat even when they're not hungry. Not only are most snacks caloric, but "not many calories are burned watching TV," Squires says. "In fact, research shows that metabolism actually declines to levels as low as during sleep." For a booby prize of a ton of French fries, what's the name we give people who routinely sit, unmoving, in front of TV with a favorite snack?

Oh, sure, you may say, *but who pays attention to commercials?* A 2006 Institute of Medicine report found that most children are strongly influenced by them. They see ads and put pressure on parents. And according to market researcher Mary Story, when children shop for groceries with parents, parents give in to kids' pleas for junk food 50 percent of the time.[37]

IS REGULATION NECESSARY?

Because of the growing problem of obesity in young people, many countries now regulate food marketing to children. For instance, "Australia bans food advertisements aimed at children

14 and younger. In the Netherlands, food companies can't advertise sweets to kids younger than 12. Sweden prohibits the use of cartoon characters to promote foods to children younger than 12." Even though the United States has fewer regulations, so many American parents and doctors have criticized TV food ads that advertisers are supposedly trying to regulate themselves.[38]

SOURCES OF FOOD INFORMATION

Although TV commercials may affect your judgment, television can also be a positive influence. Along with books, magazines, newspapers, newsletters, documentaries, and Internet websites, TV is a source of endless valuable information about food and eating habits. Maybe you're already watching programs on the Discovery or Food channels, or reading articles in *Time* or other magazines, or taking a look at medical newsletters that come to your house.

An inquiry to Amazon.com Books in the summer of 2009 showed more than 75,000 listings under "food and eating." Type in the words "food and teenagers" you'll find more than 1,500 books. Try googling "food and eating," and you'll see more than 7 million Internet references. So if you want to add books and the Internet to the list of potential influences on your eating, there are plenty of authors and bloggers who would love to influence you.

NOTES

1. "Children's Eating Habits: Parents Should Model Good Behavior," eSSORTMENT, 2–3, www.essortment.com/all/childrenseating_tvzn.htm (accessed March 26, 2008).

2. "Eating Problems: How to Handle the Picky Eater," MotherNature.com, www.mothernature.com/Library/Bookshelf/Books/50/45.cfm (accessed March 20, 2008).

3. Kim Severson, "Picky Eaters? They Get It from You," *New York Times*, October 10, 2007, F4.

4. Severson, "Picky Eaters?" F4.

5. Tara Parker-Pope, "6 Food Mistakes Parents Make," *New York Times*, September 15, 2008, H2.

6. Paul Rozin, "Sociocultural Influences on Human Food Selection," in *Why We Eat What We Eat: The Psychology of Eating*, ed. Elizabeth D. Capaldi (Washington, DC: American Psychological Association, 2004), 254.

7. Adam Drewnowski, "The Behavioral Phenotype in Human Obesity," in Capaldi, *Why We Eat What We Eat*, 292.

8. Deirdre Barrett, *Waistland* (New York: W. W. Norton, 2007), 139.

9. Rozin, "Sociocultural Influences on Human Food Selection," 254–55.

10. "Change in Taste Preferences over the Years," Chowhound: For Those Who Live to Eat, January 8, 2007, 2, www.chowhound.com/topics/358194 (accessed March 8, 2008).

11. Leon Rappoport, *How We Eat: Appetite, Culture, and the Psychology of Food* (Toronto: ECW Press, 2003), 34.

12. Rozin, "Sociocultural Influences on Human Food Selection," 235.

13. Marvin Harris, *Good to Eat: Riddles of Food and Culture* (New York: Simon & Schuster, 1985), 16.

14. Bell and Valentine quoted in Peter Scholliers, ed., *Food, Drink and Identity: Cooking, Eating and Drinking in Europe since the Middle Ages* (New York: Oxford University Press, 2001), 4.

15. E. N. Anderson, *Everyone Eats: Understanding Food and Culture* (New York: New York University Press, 2005), 84–86.

16. Anderson, *Everyone Eats*, 86–87.

17. Anderson, *Everyone Eats*, 86–87.

18. Loretta Chan, "Dad's Home Cooking," in *Staring with I: Personal Essays by Teenagers*, ed. Andrea Estepa and Philip Kay (New York: Persea Press, 1997), 28–31.

19. Helen Macbeth and Sue Lawry, "Introduction," in *Food Preferences and Taste: Continuity and Change*, ed. Helen Macbeth (New York: Berghahn Books, 1997), 11.

20. Rappoport, *How We Eat*, 72–73.

21. Reay Tannahill, *Food in History* (New York: Three Rivers Press, 1988), 124.

22. Tannahill, *Food in History*, 54–55.

23. Rappoport, *How We Eat*, 110–11.

24. Ruth A. Waihel, "Religion and Dietary Practices," FAQs.org, www.faqs.org/nutrition/Pre-Sma/Religion-and-Dietary-Practices.html (accessed April 16, 2008).

25. Rappoport, *How We Eat*, 15.

26. Waihel, "Religion and Dietary Practices."

27. Jeremy MacClancy, *Consuming Culture: Why You Eat What You Eat* (New York: Henry Holt, 1992), 35–36.

28. Stephanie V. Siek, "A Different Kind of Camp," *Boston Globe*, April 6, 2006, www.boston.com/news/local/articles/2006/04/06/a_different_kind_of_camp?mode=PF (accessed April 27, 2008).

29. Rappoport, *How We Eat*, 54.

30. Anderson, *Everyone Eats*, 135.

31. Rappoport, *How We Eat*, 55.

32. Kim Severson, "What's for Dinner? The Pollster Wants to Know," *New York Times*, April 16, 2008, F1, F5.

33. Severson, "What's for Dinner?" F1, F5.

34. Severson, "What's for Dinner?" F1, F5.

35. Michelle Strikowsky, "Food Is Most Advertised Product on TV Viewed by Kids, Study Finds," Science in the Headlines, April 17, 2007, 1, www.nationalacademies.org/headlines/20070417.html (accessed May 8, 2008).

36. Sally Squires, "Full Up to Here with Commercials," *Washington Post*, April 3, 2007, 1, www.washingtonpost.com/wp-dyn/content/article/2007/03/30/AR2007033001830.html (accessed November 27, 2009).

37. Squires, "Full Up to Here with Commercials," 1.

38. Squires, "Full Up to Here with Commercials," 1.

3 What Does Your Body Need?

If you don't eat enough, or don't eat the right stuff, your body will suffer. You'll get sick, or your growth will be affected, or, in the most extreme case, you'll die. If food is readily available to you, giving your body what it needs shouldn't be that difficult. You need essential nutrients that fall into five categories: carbohydrates, lipids (fats), proteins, vitamins, and minerals. Although you also need water, it's not usually considered a nutrient. Sometimes singly, sometimes together, nutrients accomplish three things—they give energy, build bodies, and regulate body functions.

I KNOW WHAT I SHOULD EAT, BUT . . .

Maybe you've been hearing about essential food groups since the days when you watched *Sesame Street*. "Today's teenagers have had extensive exposure to nutrition information," writes nutritionist Mary Kay Mitchell. "Nutrition is incorporated into the curriculum as early as preschool or first grade, and several studies have reported that adolescents are aware of and knowledgeable about nutrition."[1]

But a lot of teens claim they haven't been taught nutrition. For example, Alicia, age sixteen, says, "Honestly, I can't think of a single class I've had in school that has really affected my diet or how I think of food. In second or third grade I think we may have discussed it in health class, but I really don't remember it. In health class in high school we watched some overdramatic movies on eating disorders, but I don't know anyone who took them seriously."

WHERE DID YOU GET THOSE EATING HABITS?

Kat Malek, age seventeen, explains how she eats.

I think my eating habits have definitely been influenced by my parents, for the not-so-good and for the good. They don't always eat healthy, which has made me want to eat healthy and watch my weight. I sometimes have sugar cravings like any other teenager, but I have learned that eating healthy food makes me feel better and is better for me. I think I have influenced my parents to buy healthy foods for the house and to cook healthy foods, which is good for them too.

My dad has definitely helped me lately, because he has done research and will cook me something healthy when I'm hungry. Another thing is that one of my closest friends and I have formed a sort of support group. When we feel like eating something unhealthy we help each other figure out a better alternative. This really works for me because it's nice to know I'm not the only one doing it. We always allow each other a break once in a while with a sweet item, because otherwise we would not be able to keep it up.

And Kimmy, age seventeen, says, "We received the food pyramid in Home Ec, but it was only really mentioned in passing, and we were expected to already understand it."

Even if you were taught about nutrition, you might be forgetting or ignoring whatever you learned that was useful. Teenagers participating in a Rand Youth Poll indicated that they were aware of the importance of eating breakfast, and yet a later survey showed that two-thirds of participants ate limited breakfasts or none at all.

"I grab an apple or some M&Ms on my way out the door sometimes. I love breakfast and would love to have time to sit down and start my day off right, but I always seem to be too rushed in the morning. I don't think eating breakfast makes me feel any different than when I don't eat it."

—Kimmy, age seventeen

In general, surveys indicate that no matter how well informed teens are, they're likely to skip meals, eat unbalanced meals, and indulge in unhealthy snacks.[2]

Kat says, "One of my closest friends and I have formed a sort of support group."

A lot of teenagers—and adults, too—ignore healthy-eating advice out of ignorance, laziness, or rebelliousness, but some perfectly well-intended young people eat carelessly because they're confused. How do you know whose advice to follow? Doctors, nutritionists, and food writers don't always agree about which foods, or eating practices, are best. For instance, some may believe a substantial breakfast is essential and others may think skipping breakfast is no big deal. And sometimes when experts do seem to agree on, let's say, "margarine is healthier than

USDA DIETARY GUIDELINES FOR AMERICANS[3]

1. **Eat a variety of foods.** Lean toward *whole-grain* products, *fiber*-rich fruits and vegetables, and *low-fat* dairy products.

    Whole-grains are found in bread (bagels, pita, crackers), some cereals, pastas, rice, and other carbohydrates. *Fiber* is a mix of substances found in plant cell walls. It's found in oats, brown rice, dried beans, seeds, carrots, corn, sweet potatoes, apples, oranges, and other fruits. *Low-fat* is defined as "three grams or less of fat per serving."

2. **Eat nutrient-dense foods,** ones rich in vitamins and minerals but with relatively few *calories*. Limit intake of *saturated* and *trans fats*, added sugars, *cholesterol* and salt, all of which are found in many commercially prepared foods. *Calories* are the amount of energy provided by food. All foods have calories. The number is determined by burning food in a calorimeter and measuring heat produced. Fat contains more calories per gram than carbohydrates and protein. To maintain your best weight and feel energetic, take in just the number of calories your body needs. *Saturated* and *trans fats* are the ones to avoid. *Cholesterol*, measured in milligrams, is a waxy substance made by your liver. Your body needs it to form essential compounds. However, extra cholesterol that you take in (from all animal-related foods and beverages such as meats, eggs, cheese, and milk) gets stored in your arteries and clogs them with a fatty deposit called plaque. Many foods labeled "no cholesterol" still have a lot of calories.

3. **Maintain a healthy weight** for your size and build. Most teenage girls require daily about 2,000 calories and boys about 2,600+, depending on level of activity. Engage in physical exercise most days.

4. **Limit your intake of fat** to no more than one-third of your daily calorie count (that is about 600–800 fat calories for females, 900+ for males). Eat lean meats and poultry and unsaturated, low-in-cholesterol fats, such as those found in fish, nuts, and vegetable oils.

5. **Limit the amount of *sodium*** (salt) you consume. Daily intake should be less than 2,300 milligrams—about one teaspoon of table salt.

6. **Get enough *potassium*, fiber, and *vitamins A, C, and E*.** *Potassium* is a mineral needed for pH balance and for water balance, muscle growth, and brain function. Bananas are an excellent source. Other good sources are most fruits and vegetables, soy products, and fish. *Vitamin A* promotes good vision and healthy skin, bones, teeth, and mucous membranes. It's found in carrots and other beta-carotene-rich foods such as orange-yellow fruits and vegetables as well as dark green vegetables. *Vitamin C* (ascorbic acid) helps keep your bones, teeth, and blood vessels healthy; helps heal wounds and boost your resistance to infection; and participates in the formation of collagen. Foods that provide vitamin C include melons, berries, citrus fruits, mangoes, tomatoes, and yellow peppers. *Vitamin E* is important for health of red blood cells, muscles, and other tissues. Vitamin E–rich foods include vegetable oils, whole-grain cereals, green leafy vegetables, nuts, peanut butter, and wheat germ.

7. **Make sure you get enough *iron*—**especially important for females. *Iron* is a mineral your body needs to make sure your muscles receive enough oxygen. Iron deficiency can make you sluggish, irritable, and headachy. Good sources are lean red meats, other meats, egg yolks, liver, beans, green vegetables, nuts, and wheat germ.

8. **If you aren't a milk drinker,** find other sources for *calcium* and the many other nutrients provided by milk. *Calcium*, the most abundant mineral in your body, is essential for health of bones and teeth. Best sources are yogurt, milk, hard cheeses, sardines, and calcium-fortified foods. Recommended amount in milligrams for teens is about 1,300 per day.

butter," they reverse their opinion when research turns up new information. We have to expect some revisions, of course, but with all the food news that is pumped out by doctors, journalists, and others, it's hard to separate food nonsense from food sense.

WHERE'S THE ADVICE COMING FROM?

For starters, be aware of the backgrounds and motives of those who are giving you food information. Is the person a doctor, nurse, nutrition researcher, government employee, teacher, writer, celebrity, or what? Regardless of which category, note his or her training and experience, but no matter how impressive, don't give anyone a free pass. Most medical doctors have only your good health in mind when they give advice on eating. But in a few cases doctors with selfish motives have become rich from dispensing diet pills and/or selling diet books.

Experts in nutrition—teachers or others who conduct food studies—may be less likely than doctors to be drawn into the money-and-fame game, but even they, occasionally, have some sort of bias. When you consult nutritionists about food choices, try to judge the thoroughness and sensibleness of their research. For example, are they basing an opinion on a study of 10 people or 10,000, and how, where, and when has that study been conducted? Are these nutritionists willing to listen to alternative opinions, or do they insist that they have the one true way?

WHAT IS OUR GOVERNMENT'S INVOLVEMENT?

Since it's obviously good for a country if its citizens are healthy, our government has become involved in dispensing nutrition information. Since 1980 the U.S. Department of Agriculture (USDA) and the U.S. Department of Health and Human Services have been collaborating on the *Dietary Guidelines for Americans* of all ages. An adapted version of their updated recommendations appears here.

Can we trust completely the advice of food scientists who work for the government? Most of them surely want us to be healthy, but critics claim that the USDA guidelines are sometimes worded to protect certain financial interests. For instance, if the guidelines were to state openly "Eat less meat," the whole meat-producing industry would rise up in arms. So, by leaving out the word *meat* and instead advising us to "choose the right fats," writers of guidelines may be hoping to avoid hassles with big business.

CAN YOU TRUST FOOD WRITERS?

Anybody can write about food. You yourself could claim to be an expert. So if you want to feel confident about advice from someone who is primarily a writer, ask a person you trust to recommend books, articles, and websites. If a claim in these sources seems far-fetched or controversial, look for confirmation in a second or third source. If you go online, look for websites posted by universities (websites with a domain name ending in .edu), scientific journals, or governmental agencies (domain ending in .gov). Occasionally an unlikely source might provide a nugget of good information, but generally speaking, which seems more reliable to you—a recognized Internet source such as www.health.harvard.edu/ newsletters/Harvard_Health_Letter.htm, or a site (this one is invented) like www.skinnygirl.com?

If skinnygirl and hunkyguy are your favorite celebrities, you probably won't care what their nutritional qualifications are. If gorgeous or charismatic celebrities can get you to eat well, more credit to them. In short, use good sense in evaluating advice that celebrities offer, even in unpaid interviews. And when celebrities are obviously being paid to promote certain food products, try to avoid being dazzled by charisma and pretty faces.

In the end, no matter how good the sources, who has time to digest so much food information? Almost no one. Which leaves us with the options of eating carelessly and feeling guilty all the time, slavishly following a particular diet plan, or going with the guidelines that will keep cropping up in this book—namely, eat mostly *food* rather than processed products; lean toward fruits, vegetables, and whole grains; eat side-dish portions of meat and fish; include, in small amounts, whichever foods you most enjoy.

WHEN DID EATING GET SO COMPLICATED?

Cavemen and cavewomen didn't consult anybody about what to have for dinner. They considered themselves lucky to find or catch something edible in the wild. Until recently, parents passed down food ways from their parents to their children, and almost nobody read a book or consulted an expert in order to decide what to eat. But in the last decades, Michael Pollan says in *In Defense of Food*, parents lost a lot of authority over the family diet and handed it over to scientists, food marketers, and, to some extent, the government "with its ever-shifting dietary guidelines, food-labeling rules, and perplexing pyramids."[4]

And when did we start counting grams of fat and taking vitamin supplements? According to Pollan, there was no single event that made us shift from eating food to eating nutrients,[5] but in the late 1960s, because of a big increase in the United States in chronic illnesses related to diet, a government committee set up dietary goals for Americans. The committee's main purpose was to help us ward off heart disease, cancer, and diabetes.

The resulting USDA *Dietary Guidelines for Americans*, first published in 1980 and revised every five years, have been useful but imperfect. The imperfections have to do with disagreements among scientists, wording that favors some groups over others, and too much focus on separate nutrients rather than on whole foods. It's not just governmental agencies, of course, that have made our food choices complicated. Manufacturers and sellers of processed foods have made big profits from these complications.

WHO STARTED ALL THIS ANALYZING?

You and your friends may be used to daily conversations about fats and carbs, even though your ancestors had no idea what those terms meant. It all started in the early nineteenth century, when an English doctor-chemist, William Prout, identified the three principal constituents of food (macronutrients)—protein, fat, and carbohydrates. Then a German scientist named Justus von Liebig identified certain minerals. Building on the work of these two, other scientists discovered the first set of micronutrients, which Polish biochemist Casimir Funk called *vitamins*. Obviously these components were present in food all along, but it wasn't until the 1900s that scientists figured out how to isolate them, how they complemented each other, and how they functioned in the human body.

WHAT HAPPENS WHEN YOU EAT?[6]

◎ **Your digestive system is a series of hollow organs joined in a twisting tube from the mouth to the anus. In the mouth, stomach, and small intestine, a lining called the mucosa contains tiny glands that produce digestive juices. Two solid organs, the liver and pancreas, produce digestive juices that reach the intestine through small tubes. Nerves and blood also contribute to digestion.**

◎ **In the first stage of chemical breakdown, you chew food so that it mixes with saliva.**

◎ **When you swallow, food moves through your esophagus to your stomach, where three things happen. Your stomach stores partially digested food and liquid, mixes it with its own juices, and sends it on to the small intestine.**

◎ **In the small intestine further breakdown occurs (assisted by juices from the pancreas and liver). Digested nutrients, absorbed through the intestinal wall into the bloodstream, are carried to your cells for the purpose of maintaining your body and giving you energy. Meanwhile, waste products go on to your colon, where they remain, usually for a day or two, until you have a bowel movement.**

IN A NUTSHELL—WHAT YOUR BODY NEEDS

◎ *Carbohydrates*, simple or complex. Simple carbs are found in fruits, honey, and milk. Complex carbohydrates, also known as starches, are found in whole grains, pasta, potatoes, beans, and vegetables. Carbs provide energy.

◎ *Fats*, found in oils of fruit, vegetables, and nuts and in meat, dairy products, poultry, and fish. Fats provide energy, promote growth, protect vital organs, and provide a layer of insulation.

◎ *Proteins*, composed of amino acids. Proteins are nonessential (those your body can generate) and essential (those you can get only from what you eat). Protein-rich foods include meat, poultry, fish, seafood, tofu, dairy products, and eggs. Proteins build and repair the body, carry nutrients to cells, and regulate body processes.

◎ *Vitamins*, such as A, B, C, D, E, and K. Vitamins help your body process carbs, fats, and proteins. They also aid in the workings of the blood, hormonal, and nervous systems and prevent diseases. Fresh, natural foods contain more vitamins than processed foods.

◎ *Minerals*, including calcium, magnesium, and phosphorus for bones and teeth, and sodium, potassium, and chloride for helping to regulate water and chemical balance. You need at least twenty-two, some, like iron and copper, in trace amounts.

◎ *Fiber*, soluble and insoluble. Fiber is the part of plant foods that doesn't get absorbed. Soluble fiber, found in citrus fruits, strawberries, and oatmeal, helps lower blood cholesterol, whereas insoluble fiber (whole-grain bread, many vegetables, and cereals) helps prevent constipation.

NUTRITIONISM

So naming and analyzing the components of food was a useful thing, right? Generally, yes. And since that time scientists have become more and more sophisticated in their work. According to Michael Pollan and other critics, maybe *too* sophisticated for our own good. Pollan certainly doesn't object to nutritional research. He's just suspicious of "nutritionism," as opposed to nutrition. The difference is that good nutrition is providing our bodies with what they need for growth and energy, and nutritionism is a belief, not a science.

Nutritionism is a vague belief that foods are the sum of their "invisible, slightly mysterious nutrient parts," and that, given this mysteriousness, we poor, confused eaters need the help of scientists and journalists to tell us what—and exactly how much of it—to eat. Pollan and others critical of nutritionism are urging us to get nutrients from whole foods rather than from processed foods. What's the difference? Whole foods come from nature. Processed foods are packaged, food-like substances with added ingredients that almost no one can pronounce.[7]

PROCESSED FOODS

"My eating habits are probably pretty atypical for someone my age. I try really hard to avoid fast foods and extremely processed food as much as I can."

—Amy, age nineteen

Fruit off the tree, vegetables from the ground, fish from the stream are *not* processed. Processed foods have had something done to them to change their natural form. Although there may be a slight nutritional loss in foods that have been pasteurized, dried, frozen, or canned, these types of *light* processing extend the life of a food and don't do harm. *Heavy* processing, however—as in the case of frozen dinners, sugared cereals, chips, cookies, Twinkies, and thousands of other products—results in three negatives: (1) loss of nutritional value, (2) extra calories from fats and sugars, and (3) the addition of unwholesome additives.[8]

Amy says she avoids "extremely processed food." The reason she clarifies is that most foods, including staples we eat every day, such as refined bread and rice, are processed to some extent. Most chickens these days have been given antibiotics. Most cows have been raised on chemical feed. Avoiding even lightly processed foods would be very limiting and probably not a requirement for good health.

Do you drink orange juice with calcium added? Sometimes valuable nutrients are added in the processing. In defense of lightly processed foods, they can be distributed more widely because they last longer than fresh foods. The question remains though, whether the convenience of processed foods outweighs their disadvantages.

Processed Foods Get a Grip on Us

Your great (or at least your *great*-great) grandma never heard of fast foods. She never microwaved a pizza. She didn't know about breakfast bars, or chicken nuggets, or take-out tacos, or sugar-loaded sodas. The great leap from grandpa's growing corn in the backyard to agri-complexes producing tons of corn on thousands of acres was accomplished all in the last few decades.

Over the last century or so, advanced farm machinery and irrigation made it possible to grow more food more easily. Scientific advances such as chemical fertilizers, pesticides, and safer storage resulted in increased food production. These changes were helpful for the most part, given the needs of an ever-increasing population.

If you live in or near an urban area, you may visit a farm once a year or so, maybe on an outing to pick apples or pumpkins. That's because small farms and other family-run food producers have often merged into, or lost out to, big companies. Big companies, eager to build profits, keep on looking for ways to sell as much food as possible. Never mind if more food is produced than we need to satisfy hunger. The attitude of big companies remains the same: Sell people more than they need! Create new needs for more profit!

TOO MUCH

Do you know people who buy and eat more than they need? Unfortunately most of us keep on being tempted even when we're full. If we can afford tasty extras, most of us buy and consume them. The reason why a lot of these tasty caloric foods are so affordable can be traced to changes in U.S. agricultural policy during the Nixon presidency (1969–1974). By 2000, farmers were producing 600 more calories per person per day than in 1980.[9] These new processed products, mostly derived from corn, were relatively cheap in comparison with fresh foods, so people began to buy more and more processed foods.

Even back then, consumers found out about new foods the same way we do today—from ads. Starting with the time

🍴 "I LITERALLY CRINGE"

Amy Torres, a nineteen-year-old college student, works in the summer at Bischoff's ice cream shop in Teaneck, New Jersey.

The perks of working in a place known for its ice cream are getting to see a lot of people in the community and getting a good discount. The most common reaction I get from customers is comments on how large the portions are.

A downside is having to throw out so much food and ice cream every day. It's really hard to see how much effort goes into cooking food and then to see how much of it goes into the garbage. When parents allow their kids to order huge sundaes, I literally cringe, already predicting how more than half will end up in the garbage.

when most American families owned at least one TV set (in the 1950s), food advertisers had access to bigger audiences than ever. These audiences included many eaters who started preferring refined and otherwise processed foods.

Why did sliced white bread, for instance, beat out healthier whole-grain loaves? Because lots of people came to prefer the

Amy Torres likes her summer job in an ice cream shop, but she hates to see wasted food.

taste and texture of white bread and came to associate it with richness and refinement. Food producers, then and now, are happy about that preference, because additives in white bread give it longer shelf life, which translates into less waste and more profit for them.

TV ADS AND MORE ADS

"I always want Coke after I see Coke ads. Also, Olive Garden commercials give me cravings. I eat a certain energy bar during my tennis matches because my favorite tennis player eats them."
—Kimmy, age seventeen

Through the years, commercials on television have promoted processed foods. Think about the ads you've seen in the roughly twenty-one hours a week you watched TV, if you were an average kid. Did any commercials then, or now, encourage you to eat fresh apples and carrots? Obviously not, because there's more profit for marketers in selling you on heavily processed breakfast cereals, snack foods, and fast foods. Fast food chains, by the way, spend about $3 billion annually on television advertising.[10] Those billions apparently pay off, since a recent study showed that "teens viewed approximately 17 food ads per day or over 6,000 a year, 80 percent of those ads for fast foods and junk foods."[11]

In other words, processed foods have become popular because ads convince people to like them—and because they're affordable. Food producers love processed foods because they bring in more profits than basic fruits and vegetables. Also, in an affluent society, lots of people will pay for convenience, and frozen items are quicker and easier to prepare than slow-cooked meals.

WHY PACKAGED FOODS ARE POPULAR

Along with our love of convenience and novelty, many Americans are obsessed with dieting. Processed, packaged foods with "nutrition facts" and labels claiming "low carb" or "fat free" may seem like just the thing to ensure healthy eating. No question, food labeling is useful. It can be an aid to eating wisely. But if labels are overwhelming, misleading, or confusing, they aren't very useful. Bottom line: How come, with so many food choices and such good access to nutrition labels, two-thirds of Americans are overweight or obese?[12]

WHO'S AT RISK?

Because medical science has made huge leaps, most people these days live longer and many are healthier. Still, at the same time that certain contagious diseases such as tuberculosis and measles have been controlled, obesity is on the rise, along with illnesses often connected to diet, such as stroke, heart disease, diabetes, cancer, and osteoporosis. Who is most vulnerable to these diseases? Regardless of where in the world they live, people who follow the pattern known as the Western diet—that is, people who eat "lots of processed foods and meat, lots of added fat and sugar, lots of everything except fruits, vegetables, and whole grains."[13]

What is it about the Western diet that causes health problems? The answer isn't simple, because nutrients work together rather than in isolation. Still, the above-mentioned diseases are most often found in people who consume a lot of fat, refined sugar, and sodium, and not enough calcium, so it's clearly smart to keep your weight down and to limit salt intake.

WESTERN DIET

If you need to be convinced that a diet of high-fat, refined, processed foods isn't good for you, take a look at evidence accumulated for the last 100 years. Back in the 1930s a Canadian dentist, Weston Price, suspected that his American patients, including kids, were "malnourished on industrial foods." To prove a point he studied "preindustrial" communities around the world where there wasn't much chronic illness or tooth decay. But when these people, from New Guinea to Ireland and beyond, changed their diets and ate "sugar and jam, white flour and white rice, and refined vegetable oils . . . their health declined sharply."[14] His conclusion was to recommend whole foods, especially grains; and to cut down on refined flour and sugar.

Back to the Bush

What would happen if you were sent to live in the woods for seven weeks, to eat only what you could find there? In 1982, a nutritional researcher in Australia, Kerin O'Dea, located ten "middle-aged, overweight, and diabetic Aborigines who had all contracted health problems after leaving the bush." These men, who had grown up eating fish, birds, turtle, fruits, and vegetables, after a number of years of eating processed and refined foods began to exhibit obesity, high blood pressure, and diabetes.

Her experiment required the Aborigines to return to the bush for seven weeks. During that time they weren't allowed any store-bought food or beverages, and they were allowed to eat only what they found in the wild, including kangaroo, grubs, figs, and bush honey.

End of story: Blood drawn by O'Dea from the Aborigines showed that in seven weeks, all had better blood pressure and triglyceride levels, as well as fewer abnormalities associated with diabetes, and all had lost weight (an average of 17.9 pounds).[15]

Western Diet Takes Over

Leap ahead to the present. Studies of Pima, Sioux, and other Native Americans indicate that those groups experience great weight gain when they give up traditional hunting and gathering and rely on consumption of white flour, potatoes, and canned milk.[16]

And it's not just Americans who are risking their health by dependence on the Western diet. Even in Greece, formerly known for its healthy Mediterranean cuisine of goat's milk, bread, honey, fresh produce, and fish, and where many people used to live to 100, the diseases of civilization are rampant. With the arrival of "chocolate shops, pizza places, ice cream parlors, soda machines, and fast-food joints," two-thirds of children are now overweight and, instead of sniffles and stomachaches, pediatricians are treating them for diabetes, high blood pressure, and high cholesterol.[17]

Ironically, at the same time that 800 million people in the world are hungry, they are outnumbered by the *1 billion* people in the world who are overweight. According to food policy analyst Raj Patel, "Global hunger and obesity are symptoms of the same problem." Changing the worst features of food production could, at the same time, end world hunger and prevent epidemics of diabetes and heart disease.[18]

The big question is, How far are we willing to go change our personal eating habits?

WANT A LONG LIFE?

Even though a long life isn't necessarily the best life, if you'd like to be around in the next century, consider the fact that those who live longest eat differently from the way most Americans eat. Which country wins the longevity prize? Andorra, a little country in the Pyrenees Mountains between France and Spain, has the longest life expectancy, and it's followed by Japan, Macau, San Marino and Singapore.[19] One thing that these places have in common is that kids aren't swilling down sodas or eating sugar-coated cereals.

OBESITY IS PREVENTABLE

"The real tragedy is that overweight and obesity and their related chronic diseases are largely preventable," says Robert Beaglehole, World Health Organization director of chronic diseases and health promotion. "Approximately 80% of heart disease, stroke, type 2 diabetes, and 40% of cancer could be avoided through healthy diet, regular physical activity and avoidance of tobacco use."[20]

FOOD-RELATED ILLNESS AND HOW TO AVOID THEM

Heart disease. Along with smoking, high blood cholesterol levels are contributors to heart disease. It's good to routinely have your blood cholesterol levels checked. If they're high, you'll be advised to eat less animal fat and switch to low-fat dairy products. Even though researchers don't all agree that animal fat necessarily causes illness,[21] reducing fat in your diet makes sense if you want to play it safe.

High blood pressure. Overweight people often have high blood pressure, which may lead to stroke—a blockage or rupture of a blood vessel in the brain. Consuming too much salt can raise blood pressure. Statistics show that 40 to 50 percent of adults in the United States are at risk of developing high blood pressure.[22]

Diabetes. Diabetes is a condition that affects the way the body uses energy from sugar, starch, and other foods. It occurs when not enough of the hormone insulin is produced in the pancreas, resulting in problems with metabolism. Type 2 diabetes (90 to 95 percent of all cases—often found in overweight people who don't exercise much) can sometimes be controlled through diet, weight control, and exercise. Otherwise, injections of insulin may be needed to head off serious effects of the disease, such as blindness, circulatory problems, and nerve and kidney disease.

Diabetes affects about 21 million Americans, including a growing number of children and teenagers. Type 1 diabetes, usually diagnosed in children and young adults, is more common among whites than people of color. Type 2, usually diagnosed in adults, is found more often in people of color than in whites. Early detection by way of urine and blood tests is very important.[23] See the sidebar in which teens talk about coping with diabetes.

Cancer. Limiting your consumption of animal fats and making a point of eating fruits and vegetables high in antioxidants (found in fresh, brightly colored fruit, berries, and vegetables) may protect you from cancer. "The same high-fat diet associated with heart disease also may increase the risk of developing certain cancers. . . . Among the Japanese, who eat little fat of any kind, breast and colon cancers are uncommon."[24]

Osteoporosis. If you have too little calcium in your diet, you may be vulnerable to osteoporosis, which causes bone shrinkage, bone fractures, and dental problems. Osteoporosis occurs earlier and more often in women than in men, but males, too, are vulnerable as they age. Although calcium can be taken as a supplement, it's absorbed better by the body when it comes directly from foods such as dairy products and green vegetables.

53

COPING WITH DIABETES[25]

Mikaela Carillo, age thirteen: "I have to check my blood sugar all the time. Even though everyone says diabetics can't eat sugar, that's not exactly true. It's more the carbohydrates. They turn into sugar; so you just have to count your carbohydrates each day and keep track of your insulin. I'm on an insulin pump. I give myself insulin according to what I eat."

Quinn Nystrom, age sixteen: "I'm a typical teenager, except I have an incurable disease. I am one of 17 million Americans with diabetes. Thanks to insulin, I can lead an almost normal life.

"That summer [of diagnosis] my parents forced me to go to diabetes camp in Hudson, Wisconsin—and I mean FORCED! . . . I did not want to go and spend a week talking about diabetes. . . . But camp was a turning point for me. It was full of kids just like me, struggling with the same things. It felt great to be part of the crowd and not the only one who had to sneak off and give myself a shot."

Evie Taylor, age nineteen: "I was diagnosed with Insulin Dependent Diabetes (Type 1) at age 11. It could not have been prevented. It is an autoimmune disease treated with daily multiple injections of insulin. I am now 19 years old and attending my local college. . . . Diabetes has never prevented me from enjoying life to the fullest. . . . While normal activities, like eating, are sometimes difficult, I never let them hold me back. I just take it for what it is and go on."

IS A LITTLE EXTRA WEIGHT SO BAD?

Researcher David Allison found that about 300,000 Americans die each year because they weigh too much. One of his colleagues claimed that the number of premature deaths each year was even higher. But when their colleagues, Katherine Flegal, a statistician, and David Williamson, a specialist in epidemics, checked the statistical methods of those studies, they concluded, to their own surprise, that early deaths caused by obesity weren't as numerous as reported.

In fact, indications were that "rather than being at an increased risk of death, overweight people were, if anything, better off. Their death rate was slightly lower than the death rate for so-called normal-weight people." So, even though researchers agree that there's an increased risk of early death for the very thin and very obese, statistics showed that "as far as mortality was concerned, overweight was the best weight to be."[26]

More recently, in 2007, researchers at the Centers for Disease Control and Prevention and the National Cancer Institute reported that "overweight people appear to have longer life expectancies than so-called normal weight adults."[27]

In short, research increasingly confirms that a little extra weight isn't so bad. Besides the Flegal-Williamson findings, back in the 1980s economist Robert Fogel found that as populations grew healthier they grew taller and fatter. Okay, if we're becoming taller and fatter as a society, the good news is that we're also becoming healthier.[28]

P.S. Everyone still agrees that actual obesity threatens health.

YOU'RE UNIQUE

Obviously all bodies aren't the same. Your needs aren't necessarily the same as those of your friend. Most doctors say that being a little bit overweight is nothing to worry about if you're "metabolically healthy," meaning that your cholesterol levels, blood pressure, blood sugar, and other heart-disease-risk factors are in the normal range. Another point to note is that being thin doesn't guarantee good health. One out of four slim people show risk factors having to do with heart health.[29]

If You're an Athlete

If you expend a lot of energy, you can and should eat more than less active kids eat. Kimmy says, "Tennis has made food my fuel more often than a treat. I normally eat so that my game will be better and I'll be prepared to play for several hours. Because I'm an athlete I try to stay away from extremely fattening foods or foods that might upset my stomach. I have to be aware of what I'm eating in order to take my game to the next level."

DIETARY SUPPLEMENTS

"I try to take a multivitamin every day, as well as a calcium pill whenever I remember. I take multivitamins now that I'm a vegetarian. And I've been trying to take calcium pills because I don't really ever drink milk."
—Amy, age nineteen

Let's say you're not sure if you're not eating properly, so you take a multiple vitamin pill every morning. Not a bad idea. But let's says you don't have time to eat food, so you down a

---

WATER, WATER[30]

Why do you need it?
To survive. Without it, you would last only a few days. Dehydration, of loss of body fluids, can lead to muscle spasms, a drop in blood pressure, and other serious symptoms.

What does water do for us?
Helps digest food, move food, and excrete wastes. It cushions and lubricates brain and joint tissue. It's the main component of saliva, mucous secretions, and other body fluids, and it helps regulate body temperature.

How much do you need?
On average, the equivalent of eight 8-ounce glasses per day, *including* water from other beverages, soups, fruits, vegetables, and so forth. You need enough water to replace about two to three quarts a day—maybe more in hot weather—lost through perspiring, sneezing, and urinating.

Is bottled water safer and healthier than tap water?
If your tap water comes from a municipal system, it's just as safe as bottled water. Some studies have shown that bottled water may actually have a higher bacterial count, not to mention that some bottled waters are packaged tap water. Also, most bottled waters lack fluoride, valuable for protection of teeth and bones.

How do you know if you're getting enough water?
Your urine should be light yellow. Dark yellow indicates the need to drink more.

can of protein supplement. Not smart. Most experts agree that "dietary supplements can complement your regular diet if you have trouble getting enough nutrients. But they aren't meant to be food substitutes."[31] And since vitamin pills and canned liquids can't replicate the benefits of whole foods, you may as well eat healthily instead of wasting money on supplements.

In any case, if you think you have a deficiency, consult a doctor. Information about dietary supplements is available online from the National Institutes of Health website, under "Vitamin and Mineral Supplement Fact Sheet," but this source isn't a substitute for professional medical advice.

And don't forget your body needs water. What your body doesn't need is many more calories than you burn—especially if those calories come from unnatural, heavily processed foods, foods loaded with sugar and fat. . . . Even though a little extra cushion may actually be good for your long-term survival, if you're among the millions interested in losing weight, read on.

BETTER WATER?

Andrew, age thirteen, answers the following questions: Is it better to drink bottled water, or is tap water good enough? Or is there another alternative?

I prefer filtered water over bottled water. Whenever I am at home, I always drink filtered water. We keep a pitcher of it in the fridge. It is cheaper than drinking bottled water and better for the environment.

But when I am out, I usually will have bottled water even though I know bottled water uses a lot of plastic and is very wasteful. Even the bottled water companies have noticed this. If you look carefully in different stores, you can see that some companies have designed new bottles that use less plastic and smaller labels, so that less paper is wasted. Another problem with plastic water bottles is that many animals are choking on the bottle caps and dying.

I also read in the newspaper about this town in Australia that has banned the sale of bottled water for the reasons I mentioned already. Although I know they are doing this for a good cause, it still seems a little extreme. Anyway, I always try to use filtered water at home, and when I have to drink bottled water I always recycle the bottles.

Andrew is in favor of drinking filtered—but not bottled—water.

NOTES

1. Mary Kay Mitchell, *Nutrition across the Life Span* (New York: W. B. Saunders, 1997), 176.

2. Mitchell, *Nutrition across the Life Span*, 176.

3. Material adapted from U.S. Department of Health and Human Services and U.S. Department of Agriculture, "Adequate Nutrients within Calorie Needs," in *Dietary Guidelines for Americans 2005*, 6th ed. (Washington, DC: U.S. Government Printing Office), chapter 2, www.health.gov/dietaryguidelines/dga2005/document/html/chapter2.htm (accessed May 20, 2008)

and from Joy Bauer, *Complete Idiot's Guide to Total Nutrition* (New York: Alpha Books, 2005), 4–6.

4. Michael Pollan, *In Defense of Food* (New York: Penguin Press, 2008), 3.

5. Pollan, *In Defense of Food*, 22.

6. Adapted from "Your Digestive System and How It Works," National Digestive Diseases Information Clearinghouse (NDDIC), http://digestive.niddk.nih.gov/ddiseases/pubs/yrdd (accessed February 11, 2008).

7. Pollan, *In Defense of Food*, 80.

8. Marion Nestle, *What to Eat* (New York: North Point Press, 2006), 307.

9. Pollan, *In Defense of Food*, 186.

10. Eric Schlosser, *Fast Food Nation* (New York: HarperCollins, 2002), 47.

11. Michelle Strikowsky, "Food Is Most Advertised Product on TV Viewed by Kids, Study Finds," Science in the Headlines, April 17, 2007, www.nationalacademies.org/headlines/20070417.html (accessed May 8, 2008).

12. Pollan, *In Defense of Food*, 135.

13. Pollan, *In Defense of Food*, 89.

14. Nina Planck, *Real Food* (New York: Bloomsburg Publishing, 2006), 25.

15. Pollan, *In Defense of Food*, 85–87.

16. Gary Taubes, *Good Calories, Bad Calories* (New York: Alfred A. Knopf, 2007), 235–40.

17. Elisabeth Rosenthal, "Fast Food Hits Mediterranean; a Diet Succumbs," *New York Times*, September 24, 2008, A1, A12.

18. Raj Patel, *Stuffed and Starved* (Brooklyn, NY: Melville House Publishing, 2007), 1.

19. Patel, *Stuffed and Starved*, 1.

20. Shaoni Bhattacharya, "WHO Reports Steep Rise in Obesity in Poorer Countries," NewScientist, September 23, 2005, 1, www.newscientist.com/article/dn8043-who-reports-steep-rise-in-obesity-in-poorer-countries.html (accessed November 27, 2009).

21. Pollan, *In Defense of Food*, 45.

22. Indiana 4-H, "Diet-Related Diseases," Purdue University, 1–2, www.four-h.purdue.edu/foods/Diet-Related%20Diseases%20frame1.htm (accessed June 18, 2008).

23. Roberta Larson Duyff, *Complete Food and Nutrition Guide* (New York: John Wiley & Sons, 2006), 565–67.

24. Indiana 4-H, "Diet-Related Diseases," 3–4.

25. "Diagnosed with Diabetes: Coping with a Disease That Won't Let Go," *Teen Voices* 13, no. 1 (2004): 10–12.

26. Gina Kolata, *Rethinking Thin: The New Science of Weight Loss—and the Myths and Realities of Dieting* (New York: Farrar, Straus and Giroux, 2008), 201–3.

27. Tara Parker-Pope, "Better to Be Fat and Fit Than Skinny and Unfit," *New York Times*, August 19, 2008, F5.

28. Parker-Pope, "Better to Be Fat and Fit," 206–9.

29. Parker-Pope, "Better to Be Fat and Fit," 206–9.

30. Sheldon Margen and editors of the UC Berkeley Wellness Letter, *Wellness Foods A to Z* (New York: Rebus, 2002), 606–7.

31. Mayo Clinic staff, "Dietary Supplements: Nutrition in a Pill?" MayoClinic.com, www.mayoclinic.com/health/supplements/NU00198 (accessed May 26, 2009).

4 The Great Weight Debate

How many kids do you know who would like to lose weight? Some extra pounds may be insurance when it comes to protecting health, but in most cultures these days, slimness is in. Rightly or wrongly, thinness is associated with beauty, desirability, and fashion. When American women were asked in a recent survey sponsored by the National Center for Health Statistics "Would you like to weigh less?" more than 71 percent said they would.[1]

As we've already said, even though genetics are important, you still have significant control over your body weight, and the way to slimness is making sure to burn up the calories you take in. Unless they're born with high-speed metabolisms or are serious athletes, most people have to watch what they eat. Only a few—like Olympian swimmer Michael Phelps, winner of eight gold medals—can get away with consuming 12,000 calories per day (as opposed to about 3,000 for an active teenage boy or man).

Thousands of diet books are out there. While you're reading this page, probably a few more are being published. That's why, in this chapter, we won't linger over detailed advice to dieters. Instead we'll raise questions such as, How did this obsession with weight get such a hold on us? How are we all affected by the obsession? How do we know what our ideal weight is? And what should we do if we're determined to lose—or gain—a little weight?

DID ADAM AND EVE COUNT CALORIES?

Size zero models and slim guys weren't always in fashion. Standards of beauty in the past, in the United States and elsewhere, allowed for more pounds than are considered attractive today. Our long-ago ancestors weren't sure where their next meal was coming from, so they thought of extra weight as money in the bank. And into the sixteenth century, when Henry VIII ruled Tudor England, "food was scarce and only the rich could afford to indulge themselves. A paunch was a sign of affluence, and the fashion, for men and women, was to be decidedly plump."[2]

Proof of the growing popularity of thinness over the last century is the fact that contestants in Miss America contests have gotten taller by 2 percent but slimmer by 12 percent.[3] The American preference for tall, slender, and curvy may have started with the idealized females drawn for magazines by Charles Dana Gibson at the end of the 1800s. These Gibson Girls, who influenced concepts of beauty in America and elsewhere, caused men, as well as women, to aim at being thin.

Then in the 1920s Gibson Girls gave way to even thinner "rail-thin flappers," drawn by artist John Held Jr. "These were *drawings*," says health writer Gina Kolata, "and not even drawings of real women. They were drawings of a man's fantasy of women. But they set a standard of what a woman's body should look like."[4]

HOW DID THIN BECOME SO *IN*?

How often do you step on the scale or check yourself in a mirror? Before the 1900s, it was possible not to know details about your own weight. And then, for the first time, bathroom scales and full-length mirrors appeared in American homes. As photography became more common, photos of real "ideal" women in magazines took the place of drawings, so that people began to compare themselves against real ideals. About the same time, insurance companies began insisting on knowing the weight of applicants, and they linked extra weight with high risk.

Thinness continued to be prized for both aesthetic and health reasons, and the ideal body weight continued to drop. Winners of beauty contests through the 1930s and beyond would be considered plump today. But by the 1960s the ideal female body was that of a preadolescent girl. Twiggy, a famous British model of that period, was five feet, seven inches and weighed ninety-one pounds.[5] Most people today agree that our society overvalues thinness, but since ideals of beauty change in time, maybe, one of these days, a preference for plumpness will come back.

DOWNSIDE OF WEIGHT OBSESSION

You may know kids whose lives are driven by attempts to lose weight. Maybe you yourself are unhappy when you compare yourself with an ideal. Permanent weight loss for those who are extremely overweight is very, very difficult. Medical, social, and psychological problems are even greater for the obese—those whose weight is more than 20 percent in excess of weight recommended for their height.

Is obesity a person's own fault? Scientific evidence indicates that being obese isn't just a matter of weak willpower. Nor is there evidence of an "obese personality," or strong evidence

"TIME TO REBUILD TAMYRA"[6]

Tamyra Morgan, age nineteen, tells of her experience with weight gain. Part of this struggle involved unrealistic goals she wanted to meet as a dancer.

The department store mirrors honestly reflected me from every angle, and I realized that I hated myself. Wasn't this the part that I was supposed to enjoy? This hellish experience was one that many often enjoyed—the search for a prom dress. Family and friends had donated tokens of advice for prom night. . . . I wish someone had told me to love myself. . . . However, at that age, I had yet to learn that I was most vulnerable to my own self-attacks. . . .

I sat in the middle of the fitting room floor and cried. Dance tore me down, only to make me realize that it was time to rebuild Tamyra.

that obese people are more neurotic than those of average weight. Most scientists these days agree that obesity shouldn't be thought of as a character fault.[7]

In spite of what scientists say, society's judgment is harsh. "Studies have found that fat people are less likely to be admitted to elite colleges, are less likely to be hired for a job, make less money when they are hired, and are less likely to be promoted. . . . Fat people tell researchers that they are accosted on the street by strangers who admonish them to lose weight. Often, their own children are ashamed of them. Studies have shown that even many doctors find fat people disgusting, and some refuse to treat them."[8]

In spite of the existence of groups such as the Council on Size and Weight Discrimination and the National Association to Advance Fat Acceptance, many obese people continue to feel stigmatized and unfairly blamed for their condition.

MEDIA PLAYS INTO OBSESSION

Regardless of our own body weight, we're all swamped with weight-related news and commercials. Advertisers tempt us to buy foods and beverages labeled "lite." Some try to convince us that drinking certain fortified beverages can replace normal eating. Sellers of appetite suppressants and other pills claim their products will make us eat less. Diet doctors, programs, and publications pitch us advice, plans, and materials. We're even solicited on the Internet by those who perform liposuction (removal of fat by vacuum suction) and/or bariatric surgery (reduction of the size of the stomach).

We can, of course, ignore these pitches. No one's forcing us to buy low-fat yogurt or to have our tummies suctioned. But when attention to weight comes from everywhere, all the time, most of us are affected psychologically.

"My friends and I have two different conversations about food. The first one happens when we're among those of us who are very close and trust each other. It's far more honest than the second and goes something like, 'Ah, food! I love food!' The second conversation takes place when there are other people around—boys or girls we feel self-conscious with. This one goes more like, Oh my god, I'm so fat.' Whether we think it or not, we feel that this is what we're supposed to think about ourselves."

—Alicia, age sixteen

And it isn't as if other kids are the only feeders of the obsession. Regular TV programs and glossy magazines idealize slim people, not to mention that so-called entertainment is made of weight loss. TV shows that make spectacles of obese people struggling to lose weight, have included *The Biggest Loser*, *Celebrity Fit Club*, *X-Weighted*, *Honey We're Killing the Kids*, *Bulging Brides*, and *I Can Make You Thin*.[9]

WHAT'S YOUR "RIGHT" WEIGHT?

By now you know that what's right for one person isn't necessarily right for another. If you're healthy, you feel good, and you're reasonably satisfied with your appearance, chances are you don't have to think further about your weight. In general, healthy weight means having the right amount of body fat in relation to your overall body mass. It means you have energy. Your health risks are limited. You aren't likely to age prematurely, and your quality of life is good.

The "right weight" isn't primarily about health and beauty. It's about feeling good. If you don't feel that great, if you tire easily and have a hard time moving, you may want to consider whether you're being slowed down by extra weight. Most health organizations today use BMI (body mass index) values to define healthy weight. These values aren't precise, especially if you have an unusual amount of either body fat or muscle, but knowing your BMI will show how you compare to the norm.[10]

WHAT IS BMI?

"Body mass index is a tool for indicating your weight status. The mathematical calculation takes into account both your weight and height. BMI equals your weight in pounds divided by your height in inches squared: BMI = (lb./in.) $\times$ 703."[11] If you don't feel like doing the math, search on the Internet for "body mass index." Type in your weight and height to get your BMI. A number between 18.5 and 24.9 is considered very healthy. Under 18.5 indicates underweight, and over 25, overweight. A BMI of over 30 is considered obese.[12]

WHAT'S YOUR SHAPE?

In determining ideal weight, other points to consider besides BMI are body shape and waist measurement. The location of fat on your body may indicate whether you're susceptible to diet-related illnesses. "If you carry most of your fat around your waist or upper body, you're referred to as apple-shaped. If you carry most of your fat around your hips and thighs or lower body, you're referred to as pear-shaped." In general, with regard to health, apple shape is less desirable than pear shape, because carrying fat in and around your abdominal organs increases your risk of disease.[13]

To measure your waist, find the highest point on each hipbone and measure across your abdomen just above those points. A waist measurement of more than forty inches in men or thirty-five inches in women puts you at risk, especially if your BMI is 25 or higher. If you know, or suspect, that you're overweight, it's important to consult a doctor for a complete evaluation. On the other hand, if your BMI is under 25 and you're not too heavy around the middle, there's probably no need to change your weight.[14]

OUTLOOK FOR ADOLESCENTS

Hard as it may be, getting control of weight in adolescence is crucial. Overweight teenagers often have health problems even before they reach adulthood, and 80 percent of overweight teenagers become obese adults. *Overweight*, by the way, is defined as being in the top 5 percent on recognized growth charts. Obese adults are those whose BMI is 30 or higher.

Studies conducted at the University of California at San Francisco in 2000 predict that more of today's overweight teenagers than ever will become obese by the time they're thirty-five. These obese thirty-five-year-olds will be highly vulnerable to coronary heart disease and diabetes. Other studies show that obese and overweight young people are 25 percent more likely to suffer from food allergies.[15] Although interventions along the way may help to head off illnesses, adolescence is the time to take control of weight.[16]

CONTRIBUTORS TO WEIGHT GAIN[17]

Things you probably never thought of that contribute to obesity:

1. *Sleep debt.* Too little sleep can increase body weight.
2. *Pollution.* Many pollutants affect hormones, which control body weight.
3. *Air conditioning.* Temperature control may result in burning fewer calories.
4. *Decreased smoking.* Smoking is harmful, but people who quit may eat more.
5. *Medications.* Certain drugs—contraceptives, some antidepressants, blood pressure and diabetes drugs—may cause weight gain.
6. *Ancestors' environment.* Certain recent immigrants and their offspring may be subject to influences of previous generations.
7. *Age and ethnicity of population.* People gain weight as they age. Certain non-Europeans, whose populations have increased in the United States, have a greater tendency to be obese.
8. *Childbearing.* Women tend to gain weight after giving birth.
9. *Older moms.* Babies of older mothers may have a higher risk of obesity. American women are giving birth at older ages.
10. *Unions of obese spouses.* Obese parents are predisposed to having obese children.

IF YOU WANT TO LOSE JUST A FEW POUNDS

Gaining or losing a few pounds has almost nothing to do with overall health. The main reason why you, your brother, your sister, and your grandma want to lose a few pounds is to look more attractive and fit better into your clothes. If your BMI is on the high side for your height and weight, and you'd like to drop five to ten pounds or less, there is probably no need to consult doctors or to enroll in special programs and certainly no need to consider liquid replacements or medication. A do-it-yourself-drop-down-a-size project will involve figuring out the number of calories your body needs for your particular height, weight, and level of activity; keeping track of the calories you consume; and limiting the total to a few hundred per day less than you formerly ate.

This advice, which is common knowledge and often repeated, is easy to give and hard to follow. In general, you'll have to be willing to substitute foods lower in calories for high-cal starchy dishes, desserts, snacks, and sugary beverages. You'll have to control portion size and get out of the second-helping habit. You'll be smart to move more, resist between-meal snacks, and avoid situations that lead to bingeing. Consult the "How Many Calories in . . . ?" sidebar on page 79 for calorie counts.

Getting Started

Counting each calorie is time-consuming, annoying, and unnecessary. Instead of becoming a walking calculator, try to develop an overall sense of what a day's intake should be. To get this sense, in your spare time look at basic calorie counts in this book and in other books, on Internet websites, and on packaged or restaurant foods, so that you develop a general idea of how to stay within your limit of, let's say, 1,500 or 1,800 calories a day (based on your BMI and body type).

Checking out suggested weight-loss menus in books, magazines, and websites may be helpful. Weight-loss experts often recommend limiting, but not eliminating, your favorite foods. The point here is that you aren't going to gain much by eating the occasional cookie or ice cream cone. And depriving yourself of everything you love, all the time, may cause you to give up and go wild.

A contrary view comes from diet-researcher Deirdre Barrett, who claims that radical changes are often easier. Better to skip cookies altogether than to eat one and "unleash a cascade of biochemical events. . . . It's much harder to stick with your diet the day after a lapse," she says.[18]

Meanwhile, Calories Do Count

Even though you'd like to avoid being a calorie-counting nut, checking counts now and then is informative and sometimes shocking. You might not realize that bagels have more calories than doughnuts. Or that a tuna melt contains more than 1,200 calories, or that wraps often top 800. Or, finally, that a large order of buttered popcorn at the movies represents more than half the calories most people should eat in one day.[19] Many restaurants, either because of new laws or because of customer demands, are adding dietetic choices to their menus, eliminating calories where they can, or reducing portion sizes. Eating at home, of course, allows for much more control, as long as you're willing to look at those calories charts and be influenced by them.

If you think you may be in denial about the number of calories you consume in a day, try keeping an eating journal. For a few days jot down everything—and that means *everything*—you eat. Tally up your score and find out if your head has been in the sand.

Can We Trust Calorie Counts?

You want to drop five pounds. You've gotten good at noticing calories and estimating your daily limit. Your favorite fast-food restaurant advertises diet specials—Cajun fish, let's say, at 310 calories. Sounds good. Trouble is, even in cases where reputable weight-loss organizations have endorsed fast-food meals, independent analyses of calorie counts have sometimes brought errors to light. A $5 million lawsuit was filed against both Applebee's and Weight Watchers for falsely claiming that certain Applebee's menu choices have fewer calories than they actually have.

And Applebee's isn't the only offender. The lab in Boise, Idaho, that revealed Applebee's error found similar misinformation on menus at Chili's, Taco Bell, and Cheesecake Factory.[20] Does that mean don't trust any calorie count, ever? No need to be paranoid. Most calorie information is accurate. Consider, though, that one way to be sure what you're consuming is to buy food yourself and cook it at home.

SARAH'S PORTION-SIZE RESEARCH

Sarah Galicki, as a senior at Fort Lee High School in New Jersey, got to be an Intel Science Talent Search Semifinalist on the basis of a program she devised for kids ages four to six. Her computer-based game is intended to help overweight, or "at risk," children choose appropriate portions at mealtime and snack time. The project began, Sarah says, when . . .

I was enrolled in a four-year science research class, where our ultimate goal was to find a mentor and perform an original science project. I decided on my particular area of research because of my mother. She had been diagnosed with type 2 diabetes, and I wanted to do all I could in the area of nutrition, diabetes, and obesity in order to better aid her transition in dealing with this unfortunate outcome.

During my junior year I began looking for mentors in nearby hospitals and universities. My teacher, Ms. Phyllis Citrin, helped me connect with Kathleen Keller, Ph.D., at St. Luke's Roosevelt Hospital in New York City. She was also associated with Columbia University and the New York Obesity Research Center. As her intern I spent many hours reading medical journals, writing questionnaires, and making other preparations leading up to having children attend a Child Taste and Eating Laboratory for four dinnertime visits. To summarize, the children were helped first to figure out how hungry they were and then to choose, from pictures of food on a computer, the portion size they thought would be right.

The results of my project, written up, complete with statistics and charts, showed that children as young as four to six can already determine feelings of hunger and fullness and can tell differences in portion sizes. These results made me hopeful that tools such as mine may be further developed to help overweight or "at risk" kids normalize the amount they eat.

Sarah Galicki, as a high school senior, devised a program to help overweight or at-risk kids.

"Just Half of That, Please"

You want to eat the *whole* sandwich, piece of pie, or dish of ice cream, so it's hard to call a halt. But no matter how caloric food is, if you eat just a little, you won't have a problem. Limiting portion size is the biggest challenge for those who want to be slim. Writer Mireille Guiliano says, "It's generally known that Americans on average eat 10 to 30 percent more than we need to every day."[21] Do the math. We eat, on average, 30 percent more than we need, and on average we're 30 percent above ideal weight.

"One trick I use to control my intake," Guiliano says, "is to ask myself if I can live with half the amount being offered. . . . I eat half. Slowly, of course, chewing well. . . . Contentment with most foods, in terms of taste, is to be found in the first few bites."[22]

On the other hand, nutrition professor Barbara Rollins says she's fed up with advice on eating smaller portions. "It's not big portions that make you eat more. It's big portions of calories. If you eat big portions of fruits and vegetables, they displaced other foods." In other words, a large, filling, low-cal salad will hold you much longer than a small, unfilling brownie loaded with calories.[23]

WHY YOU EAT WHEN YOU'RE NOT HUNGRY[24]

1. *It's 8 A.M. or it's noon.* Your body is conditioned to expect food at the same time each day.
2. *You see a brownie.* Brain patterns (revealed through MRIs) show a change when you see a favorite food.
3. *You smell French fries.* Scent induces the insulin secretion that makes you think you're hungry.
4. *You're cold.* Your metabolism drops when you're chilly and eating warms you up. The colder the temperature, the more you tend to eat.
5. *You had pasta for dinner.* Refined carbs cause blood sugar to drop and you may crave food again within a few hours.
6. *You crave something sweet.* After a big dinner you make room for dessert because that universal craving for sweets hasn't yet been satisfied.

What Else Can You Do?

Here are some other strategies for controlling your appetite:

1. Be consistent about mealtime. Hormone levels remain steadier if you eat on a regular schedule.
2. Slow down. Eating slowly gives your brain a chance to catch up and realize that your stomach is stretching.

3. **Consume fiber.** Eating fruits, vegetables, and other high-fiber foods helps suppress your appetite and makes you feel full.

4. **Brush your teeth.** In the middle of a meal? Well, maybe after a first small helping of ice cream. The break and the toothpaste flavor may keep you from going back for seconds.[25]

LOSING MORE THAN A FEW POUNDS

If you feel the need to lose more than ten pounds or so, see a doctor who will probably recommend a reputable weight-loss regimen. Diets are hard to evaluate on your own. Most, even if they don't work, are unlikely to hurt you, but every now and then a crazy notion has done damage to a dieter. In one case, taking a certain pill caused several fatalities and cases of blindness.[26]

Which Modern Diet Works Best?

Let's be clear from the start that even the most sensible, doctor-monitored diet is tough to follow and may not have lasting effects. Weight-loss plans usually fall into these categories: (1) low-fat diets; (2) low-carb diets; (3) glycemic-index diets, which lower blood-sugar levels; (4) meal replacements, which substitute fortified liquids for some meals; (5) meal providers—services that provide ready-made diet meals; and (6) group approaches—programs complete with support groups, weigh-ins, and so on.[27]

Can any diet, past or present, make the claim of being best? Probably not. According to diet doctor and author Dr. Sanford Siegal, "People are always looking for magic, and they're surprised when you tell them otherwise. . . . Many of the new diet schemes are actually just warmed-over fads from yesteryear, but people still want to believe." Siegal says that "celebrities can offer the worst weight-loss examples. In the mid-1970s, when Elvis Presley was squeezing into those white jumpsuits, he had reportedly tried the 'Sleeping Beauty Diet' in which he was heavily sedated for several days, hoping to wake up thinner."[28]

Famous Diets, Past and Present

Some of the many popular plans of recent years, in no special order, include the Scarsdale Diet, the Cabbage Soup Diet, the Astronaut's Diet, the F-Plan, the Zone, the South Beach Diet, the Sonoma Diet, Protein Power, Sugar Busters, the Pritikin Diet, the Blood Type Diet, the Pericault Diet, the Atkins Diet, Weight Watchers, and the Ornish Diet. In some

---

DIETING IS A MODERN THING, RIGHT?[29]

William the Conqueror, who died in 1087, got so fat that he devised his own weight-loss plan: stay in one room and consume nothing but alcohol. *The Causes and Effects of Corpulence*, by Thomas Short, was published in 1727. Other personalities in the long history of diets include

1. Sylvester Graham, minister, vegetarian, and inventor of graham crackers, who thought gluttony was not only bad for your health but also made your morally corrupt.
2. William Banting, an overweight English casket maker, whose "Letter on Corpulence," written in 1864, sold 58,000 copies.
3. San Franciscan Horace Fletcher, known as "The Great Masticator," who, around 1903, advocated incessant chewing but no swallowing.
4. Artic explorer Vilhjalmur Stefansson, who, in the 1920s, preached the benefits of imitating the Inuit diet of caribou, raw fish, and whale blubber.
5. Dr. William Hay, whose Hay Diet, in the 1930s, promoted the idea of eating all foods separately to avoid "digestive explosion."
6. Dr. Herman Teller, author in 1961 of *Calories Don't Count*. Teller sold more than 2 million books urging people to eat a high-protein diet, along with pills he provided. These safflower oil pills eventually got him convicted of mail fraud.

Outlandish diets in the past involved, in one case, taking a certain pill that caused several fatalities and cases of blindness and, in another case, taking a pill that introduced parasites into the body, so that the treatment was known as The Tapeworm Diet.

---

cases a single person takes credit for devising the plan. In others (Cabbage Soup!), the name gives a clue to which nutrients are emphasized. Often, when we read about results of a particular diet, we come away thinking, *What's the big deal? Everybody knows that.*

Still, even though diet studies are often based on small samples, some advice may be useful. For instance, the *Journal of the American Medical Association* (*JAMA*) reported on a trial showing that body shape suggested which diet would work best for individuals. People who secrete more insulin—so-called apple-shaped people—lost more weight and kept it off—on a low-carb diet than on a low-fat diet. Another report in the *JAMA* showed that "regardless of body shape, Atkins produces the greatest short-term weight loss."[30] Note the qualifier *short-term*. Atkins dieters may regain their old weight.

Other studies showed that weight loss is greater when dieters enroll in programs in which they're contacted on a regular basis by telephone or by way of interactive websites.[31] No single diet produced significantly better results than the others. And—no big surprise—dieters who lost the most weight were those who completed the full year and stuck closest to their assigned diet.[32]

TEENAGERS WHO SUCCEED

Some kids actually do lose weight and keep it off. In *Weight Loss Confidential*, dietician Anne M. Fletcher reports on 104 overweight preteens and teenagers who "lost significant amounts of weight and maintained their losses for two years or longer. The average loss was 58 pounds, with 26 of the participants having lost 75 pounds or more and 14 having lost 100 pounds or more."[33] At least 60 percent of these kids, from across the United States and Canada, came from overweight families. More than half had been overweight since age ten and many had previously tried and failed at dieting.

The explanations these teenagers gave for gaining weight in the first place included (1) too much snacking, (2) too big

WHAT IS BARIATRIC SURGERY?

Very occasionally, if someone—even a teenager—can't lose weight by means of diet and exercise, a doctor will recommend and supervise weight-loss medication or even surgery. Known as bariatric surgery, this procedure results in changes to the gastrointestinal tract, so that either intake or absorption of food is reduced.

Types of surgery include (1) stomach stapling, (2) use of a "lap band" (an adjustable gastric band that ties off part of the stomach), (3) resectioning (removing the lateral 2/3 of the stomach), and (4) implantation of a gastric stimulation device. Surgical removal of fat (liposuction) isn't classified as bariatric surgery.

"Gastric bypass is the most commonly used operation for weight loss in the United States. About 140,000 gastric bypass procedures were performed in 2005."[34] Even though results are often encouraging and this surgery is becoming safer, complications are frequent. That's why bariatric surgery should be considered only for patients with a BMI of at least 40 and should be performed with very great caution and only by highly experienced surgeons.[35]

portions, (3) not enough exercise, (4) too many sweets, (5) too much fast food, (6) eating while watching TV, and (7) eating when lonely, bored, or sad. They claimed they were motivated to lose weight in order to improve health and self-esteem, to look better, and to be able to participate in sports.

"Over and over, the teenagers told Ms. Fletcher that the motivation had come from within. Nagging parents or nasty comments only prompted many of the youngsters to eat more."[36]

How did they do it? About half did it on their own and half with the help of a health-care professional or a program, such as Weight Watchers or a summer camp for overweight teens. Aside from regular exercise, the strategies used most often included cutting back on high-fat foods, counting calories, and reducing portion size. Less frequently, dieters skipped meals, used meal replacements or weight-loss drugs, or fasted. Two with serious health problems underwent bariatric surgery.

Teen dieters, who found that keeping weight off was harder than losing it, ended up restructuring their eating habits, exercising regularly, weighing themselves weekly and cutting back if necessary, and learning more about nutrition.

NO END TO DIETING?

"I have been overweight my whole life. I'm used to being called names. . . . If anyone tells you that you're fat, say, "I am in good shape, round is a shape."

—Heather, age nineteen, who weighed 210 pounds two years ago and is now 160[37]

Have you decided not to obsess about calories? According to market researchers, fewer people are dieting now than in the 1990s. That doesn't mean they're giving up on good health or resigning themselves to obesity. They're shifting, instead, to "positive eating." That is, rather than going on deprivation diets, they're eating seasonal, home-cooked foods, including nuts, berries, avocados, olive oil, and even butter, with the result that they're enjoying what they eat and, they hope, not gaining.[38]

The reason for this shift away from strict diets, according to dietician Cynthia Sass, is that a lot of people who have tried and failed at dieting finally decide they'd "much rather focus on what to eat instead of what not to eat."[39]

Some nutritionists are skeptical about this positive-eating trend. They figure many people won't take the time to cook from scratch and others will use positive eating as an excuse to indulge.

UNDERWEIGHT

Even though nearly one in every five teens is overweight these days, a surprisingly large percentage of kids see themselves as underweight—a perception, by the way, that often isn't accurate. Males (21 percent of those in a Gallup Poll, as opposed to 16 percent of females) saw themselves as underweight, even though objective statistics indicated, for both genders, that only 4 percent were actually underweight. Guys apparently, more than girls, wish to be bigger and more buff.[40]

To be slightly underweight may be thought of as a lucky break. Eat what you want and stay slim! On the other hand, underweight is obviously dangerous if the cause is an eating disorder. Eating disorders are said to affect between 5 and 10 million of girls and women and 1 million men in the United States.[41]

Most prominent among these disorders are anorexia, which means starving yourself because you wrongly believe you are overweight, and bulimia, which involves eating huge amounts of food at a time, only to vomit it up. If you suspect you have an eating disorder, or you're concerned about a friend's extreme eating habits, don't fool around. Consult a parent, counselor, medical expert, or other responsible adult.

HOW DO YOU GAIN A LITTLE WEIGHT?

Advice to those who would like to gain a few pounds includes the following:

1. **Obviously, try to increase your calorie intake.**
2. **Instead of overeating, eat more frequently throughout the day— three well-balanced meals plus hearty snacks.**
3. **Choose nutrient-dense foods such as milk and egg whites.**
4. **Consult a doctor or dietician before taking high-protein or weight-gain supplements.**
5. **Exercise—it increases appetite.**
6. **Get enough sleep.[42]**

HOW MANY CALORIES IN . . . ?[43]

Be sure to note the exact amount. If you eat twice as much, multiply fat and calories by two!

Description	Amount	Fat in grams	Calories
All-bran cereal	1 ounce	1	70
Apple juice	1 cup	0	115
Apple, raw, unpeeled	1	0	80
Bagel, plain	1	2	200
Banana	1	1	105
Beef bouillon	1 cup	1	15
Beef steak, lean sirloin	2.5 ounces	6	150
Blueberries, raw	1 cup	1	80
Blueberry muffin	1	5	140
Bologna	2 slices	16	180
Bread stuffing	1/2 cup	15	250
Broccoli, raw cooked	1 cup	0	45
Brownies, with nuts	1	4	100
Butter	1 tablespoon	11	100
Cantaloupe	1/2	1	95
Cap'n Crunch cereal	1 ounce	3	120
Carrots, raw	1	0	30
Catsup	1 tablespoon	0	15
Cheddar cheese	1 cubic inch	6	70
Cheerios	1 ounce	2	110
Cheeseburger, 4 ounce	1	31	525
Chicken noodle soup, can	1 cup	2	95
Chicken roasted, breast	3 ounces	3	140
Chocolate chip cookies	4	9	180
Chocolate milk, low-fat	1 cup	5	180
Cola, regular	12 fluid ounces	0	160
Corn, cooked	1 ear	1	85
Cottage cheese, low-fat	1/2 cup	2	100
Cucumber with peel	6 slices	0	5
Doughnuts, cake-type	1	12	210
Eggs, hard boiled/poached	1	5	75
Flounder or sole	3 ounces	6	120
Frankfurter	1	13	145
Fruit punch, canned	6 ounces	0	85
Grapes	10	0	40
Haddock, breaded/fried	3 ounces	9	175
Ice cream, vanilla, regular	1 cup	14	270
Italian bread	1 slice	0	85
Jelly beans	1 ounce	0	105
Lettuce	1 head	0	20
Macaroni, cooked firm	1 cup	1	190
Margarine, regular, soft	1 tablespoon	11	100

(Continued)

HOW MANY CALORIES IN . . . ? *(Continued)*

Description	Amount	Fat in grams	Calories
Milk chocolate candy, plain	1 ounce	11	100
Nectarines, raw	1	1	65
Oatmeal, cooked, instant	1 packet	2	105
Olive oil	1 tablespoon	14	125
Onion rings, breaded	2	5	80
Onions, raw	1 cup	0	40
Orange	1	0	60
Orange juice	1 cup	1	110
Orange soda, regular	12 fluid ounces	0	180
Pancakes, plain (mix)	1	2	60
Peaches, canned in syrup	1 cup	0	190
Peaches, raw	1	0	35
Peach pie	1 slice	17	405
Peanut butter	1 tablespoon	8	95
Peanuts, roasted, salted	1 cup	71	840
Pears, canned in syrup	1 cup	0	190
Pears, raw	1	1	90
Pecan pie	1 pie	189	3450
Peppers, sweet, raw, red	1	0	20
Pickles, dill	1	0	5
Pizza	1 slice	9	290
Popcorn, air-popped, unsalted	1 cup	0	30
Popcorn, vegetable oil, salted	1 cup	3	55
Popsicle	1	0	70
Pork chop, pan-fried, lean	2.4 ounces	11	180
Pork bacon	3 slices	9	110
Potato chips	10	7	105
Potato, baked with skin	1	0	220
Potatoes, frozen, French fried	10 strips	8	160
Pretzels, twisted, thin	10	2	240
Prunes, dried	5 large	0	115
Pudding, chocolate, canned	5 ounces	11	205
Pumpkin pie	1 slice	17	320
Raisins	1 cup	1	435
Raspberries, raw	1 cup	1	60
Red kidney beans, canned	1 cup	1	230
Rice, brown	1 cup	1	230
Rice, white	1 cup	0	225
Roast beef sandwich	1	13	345
Rolls, commercial dinner	1	2	85
Rolls, hot dog or hamburger	1	2	115

(Continued)

HOW MANY CALORIES IN . . . ? *(Continued)*

Description	Amount	Fat in grams	Calories
Salami, cooked	2 slices	11	145
Salmon, baked	3 ounces	5	140 Shake, thick
chocolate	10 ounces	8	335
Sherbert, 2 percent fat	1 cup	4	270
Snack cakes, chocolate cream-filled	1	4	105
Spaghetti, tomato sauce, cheese	1 cup	2	190
Spinach, raw	1 cup	0	10
Strawberries, raw	1 cup	1	45
Sugar frosted flakes	1 ounce	0	110
Sugar, white, granulated	1 packet	0	25
Sweet potatoes, baked, peeled	1	0	115
Swiss cheese	1 ounce	8	105
Syrup, chocolate fudge	2 tablespoons	5	125
Taco	1	11	195
Tangerine, raw	1	0	35
Toaster pastries	1	6	210
Tofu	1 piece	5	85
Tomato, raw	1	0	25
Tuna salad	1 cup	19	375
Turkey, roasted, light and dark	1 cup	7	240
Veal cutlet, broiled	3 ounces	9	185
Vegetables, frozen, cooked	1 cup	0	105
Vinegar and oil dressing	1 tablespoon	8	70
Waffles (mix)	1	8	205
Watermelon, raw	1 cup	1	50
Wheat bread	1 slice	1	65
White bread	1 slice	1	65
Whole wheat bread	1 slice	1	70
Yellow cake, chocolate icing	1 piece	11	245
Yogurt, low-fat, fruit	8 ounces	2	230

NOTES

1. Gina Kolata, *Rethinking Thin* (New York: Farrar, Straus and Giroux, 2007), 65.

2. Kolata, *Rethinking Thin*, 66.

3. Kolata, *Rethinking Thin*, 66.

4. Kolata, *Rethinking Thin*, 74.

5. Kolata, *Rethinking Thin*, 75–78.

6. Tamyra Morgan in "Shades of Starvation: Women of Color and Eating Disorders," *Teen Voices* 12, no. 3 (2003): 13–34.

7. Kolata, *Rethinking Thin*, 90–92.

8. Kolata, *Rethinking Thin*, 67–68.

9. Alessandra Stanley, "Plus-Size Sideshow," *New York Times*, August 24, 2008, AR1.

10. Donald D. Hensrud, "Finding Your Healthy Weight," in *Healthy Weight for Everybody*, ed. Donald D. Hensrud (Rochester, MN: May Clinic Health Information, 2005), 16–17.

11. Hensrud, "Finding Your Healthy Weight," 16–17.

12. Hensrud, "Finding Your Healthy Weight," 18.

13. Hensrud, "Finding Your Healthy Weight," 18.

14. Hensrud, "Finding Your Healthy Weight," 17.

15. Nicholas Bakalar, "Food Allergies May Be Linked to Obesity," *New York Times*, May 26, 2009, D6.

16. Kirsten Bibbins-Domingo, Pamela Coxson, Mark J. Pletcher, James Lightwood, and Lee Goldman, "Adolescent Overweight and Future Adult Coronary Heart Disease," *New England Journal of Medicine* 357, no. 23 (December 6, 2007): 2371–79, content.nejm.org/cgi/content/full/357/23/2371 (accessed June 18, 2008).

17. Adapted from Brian M. Goodman, "Study Suggests 10 New Obesity Causes," CBS Evening News.com, June 27, 2006, 1–2, www.cbsnews.com/stories/206/06/27/health/webmd/main1757772.shtml (accessed August 25, 2008).

18. Deirdre Barrett, *Waistland* (New York: W. W. Norton, 2007), 6.

19. Kim Severson, "Calories Do Count," *New York Times*, October 29, 2008, D1, D9.

20. Angela Montefinise and Kathianne Boniello, "'Weight Botchers' Menu at . . . Applebee's," *New York Post*, September 28, 2008, 3.

21. Mireille Guiliano, *French Women for All Seasons* (New York: Alfred A. Knopf, 2006), 21.

22. Guiliano, *French Women for All Seasons*, 22.

23. Jeffrey Kluger, "The Science of Appetite," *Time*, June 11, 2007, 61.

24. Jeffrey Kluger, "What Makes Us Eat More," sidebar in "The Science of Appetite," *Time*, June 11, 2007, 57.

25. Kluger, "The Science of Appetite," 61.

26. Source for entire paragraph is Buck Wolf, "Belly Laughs at Early Fad Diets," ABC News.com, January 10, 2005, 1–5, abcnews.

go.com/Entertainment/WolfFiles/story?id=1537630 (accessed August 21, 2008).

27. Mayo Clinic staff, "Weight-Loss Options: 6 Common Diet Plans," MayoClinic.com, 1–2, www.mayoclinic.com/health/weight-loss/NU00616 (accessed August 26, 2008).

28. Siegal is quoted in Wolf, "Belly Laughs at Early Diet Fads," 2.

29. Wolf, "Belly Laughs at Early Fad Diets," 1–5.

30. Carolyn Sayre, "A New Diet Equation," *Time*, June 11, 2007, 68.

31. W. L. Hellerstedt and R. W. Jeffrey, "The Effects of a Telephone-Based Intervention on Weight Loss," *American Journal of Health Promotion* 11, no. 3 (January–February, 1997): 177–82, Pub Med.gov, www.ncbi.nlm.nih.gov/pubmed/10165095?ordinalpos=80&itool=EntrezSystem2.PE (accessed September 20, 2008), and V. J. Stevens et al., "Design and Implementation of an Interactive Website to Support Long-Term Maintenance of Weight Loss," *Journal of Medical Internet Research* 10, no. 1 (January 25, 2008): e1, Pub Med.gov, www.ncbi.nih.gov/pubmed/18244892?ordinalpos=14&itool=EntrezSystem2.PE (accessed September 20, 2008).

32. M. L. Dansinger et al., "Comparison of the Atkins, Ornish, Weight Watchers, and Zone Diets for Weight Loss and Heart Disease Risk Reduction: A Randomized Trial," *JAMA* 293, no. 1 (January 5, 2005): 43–53, Pub Med.gov, www.ncbi.nih.gov/pubmed/15632335?ordinaopos=13&itool=EntrezSystem2.PE (accessed September 20, 2008).

33. Quoted in Jane Brody, "104 Teenagers Who Are Role Models for Weight Loss," *New York Times*, January 16, 2007, F7.

34. "Bariatric Surgery," Wikipedia, 1–6, en.wikipedia.org/wiki/Bariatric_surgery (accessed September 20, 2008.

35. "Bariatric Surgery," 1–6.

36. Brody, "104 Teenagers Who Are Role Models for Weight Loss," F7.

37. Heather Wendel, "I'm Fat—So What?" Teen Voices Online, www.teenvoices.com/issue_current/articles/june_09_obesity2.html (accessed June 29, 2009).

38. Tara Parker-Pope, "Instead of Eating to Diet, They're Eating to Enjoy," *New York Times*, September 17, 2008, F1, F8.

39. Sass is quoted in Parker-Pope, "Instead of Eating to Diet," F1, F8.

40. Lydia Saad, "Nearly One in Five Teens Is Overweight," Gallup.com, February 13, 2006, www.gallup.com/poll/21409/Mearly-One-Five-Teens-Overweight.aspx (accessed October 4, 2008).

41. "Statistics on Eating Disorder," www.annecollins.com/eating-disorders/statistics.htm (accessed January 20, 2010).

42. "If You Are Underweight . . .," NutriTeen, www.nutriweb.org.my/nutriteen/lookgood/underweight.shtml (accessed October 4, 2008).

43. "Mike's Calorie and Fat Gram Chart For 1,000 Foods," Calorie Counters Charts.com, www.caloriecountercharts.com/chart1a.htm (accessed August 8, 2008).

5 Family Eating

Erika, age sixteen, loves to cook, especially new things, but she finds it hard to share the kitchen and wants to control whomever she is sharing with. Andrew, age fifteen, likes home-cooked dinners, particularly food seasoned with garlic, but he often finds eating with family a frustrating experience.

Parents and kids sitting down to eat dinner together on a regular basis is a rarer and rarer phenomenon in many families. Only a little more than half of kids age twelve to seventeen eat dinner with their parents five days a week or more.[1] And no surprise—as kids get older they're less likely to eat dinner with adults. Ask the older relatives in your life—if they haven't already told you a thousand times—what mealtimes were like in their early years. Are they describing whole families eating together every night—food they prepared themselves, in their own kitchens? Everybody *eating the same thing*, instead of, "You don't like this? I'll make you something else." Or "Get your own dinner." Or maybe complete silence because nobody's home.

Even back in the old days not everyone fit into the same mold, but most people today agree that eating habits have changed dramatically. These changes have come about because of two parents working, more complicated schedules for everyone, increased availability of frozen and prepared foods, takeout and affordable restaurants, and in many homes, the distraction of mealtime TV and video games.

Even today, by the way, some families are more likely than others to eat together. Information from Child Trends Data

The Fernandez family of Bogota, New Jersey, makes a habit of taking turns cooking dinner.

Bank shows that "foreign-born adolescents are more likely than native-born teens to eat meals with their families 6–7 times a week. . . . Hispanic adolescents and children are more likely than white and black teens and children to eat together 6–7 times a week. . . . Adolescents living in poverty are more likely than others to eat family meals 6–7 times a week. . . . Older teens are less likely than younger teens and children to eat with their families."[2]

NO PLACE LIKE HOME

Let's say you eat out with friends or by yourself at home. You're still getting nutrients, aren't you? What's the big deal about eating with your family? First, chances are, at home you'd be eating somewhat differently in terms of food choices and amounts. And second, a daily exchange of food and conversation with family has been shown to be good for physical and emotional health.

"Eating together as a family during adolescence is associated with lasting positive effects on dietary quality in young adulthood," according to researchers. In this University of Minnesota study, 1,500 students were surveyed in high school and then again at age twenty. Those who ate more often with their families during that period were found to be eating healthier meals on a more regular schedule. As adults they ate more fruit and vegetables; had higher daily intakes of calcium, minerals, vitamins, and fiber; and drank fewer soft drinks.[3]

Other studies, including one done at Columbia University, show that "the more often families eat together, the less likely kids are to smoke, drink, do drugs, get depressed, develop eating disorders and consider suicide, and the more likely they are to do well in school, delay having sex, eat their vegetables, learn big words and know which fork to use."[4] Eating supper with family supposedly helps keep asthmatic kids out of hospitals and discourages obesity and eating disorders. Eat with your family and lead a perfect life!

"If it were just about food," says Robin Fox, anthropologist at Rutgers University in New Jersey, "we would squirt it into their mouths with a tube. . . . A meal is about civilizing children. It's about teaching them to be a member of their culture."[5] Even if the importance of family dinners seems exaggerated in these study results, isn't it logical that family togetherness at mealtime may somehow pay off?

"In high school I ate dinner with my family every day, except when I was working or had soccer. Now that I'm away at college, I eat with my family almost every day that I'm home. I do this both because I get good quality time with them and because I'm now less willing to spend money on outside food."

—Amy, age nineteen

In spite of studies that recommend families eating together, some parents are skeptical—or perhaps defensive. Family meals and happy, healthy teens may strongly correlate, they agree, but families that are unable to eat together can also be happy and functional.

DOES TV AFFECT FAMILY MEALS?

"Turn that thing off!" Parents, nutritionists, and others often argue in favor of turning off television during family meals. But researchers at the University of Minnesota were surprised to find that "families who watched TV at dinnertime ate just about as healthfully as families who dined without it. The biggest factor wasn't whether the TV was on or off, but whether the family was eating together."[6] Researchers concluded that even though TV during dinner isn't ideal, having it on can be justified if it brings everyone to the dinner table,

Are family meals sliding further into the abyss? No. The Columbia University study showed that a greater percentage of kids age twelve to seventeen reported eating dinner with families in 2005 compared with 1998.[7] And Minnesota's Project Eat indicates that 79 percent of teenagers interviewed said they enjoyed sharing meals with their families.[8]

ANYTHING *YOU* CAN DO?

You see the advantage of shared meals and already enjoy them. Great. Or you like family meals but they don't happen very often, and you alone don't have the means to change your parents' schedules and style. In that case, maybe there isn't much you can do. But if it's *your* crazy schedule that's messing up dinnertime, you might consider changing, especially if the rest of the family is home and wishing you were there. It may be tough—perhaps impossible—to rearrange practices, rehearsals, work schedules, or homework, and you may find it even more painful to shorten time spent with friends. But give some thought to the possibility that, as you gain influence with age, you may try using that influence to improve your family's meals.

STRESSFUL MEALS

Even when a family gathers, there's no assurance of good cheer and unity. Your father may be late. Mom's disappointed that nobody likes what she cooked—or ordered in. Your brother is sullen. Your sister's hogging the conversation. You're texting under the table and figuring how to skip out before cleanup time.

Or else your family is just you and one other overburdened, tired person. Maybe that person is thinking, like the blogging "Single Ma," "First I have to pay over $100 for one week's worth of groceries. Then I have to come home to a mouthy teenager."[9] So is it less stressful to give up on eating together and go your separate ways? Not according to writer Miriam Weinstein, who says in *The Surprising Power of Family Meals*, "Research shows that even families who are toxic, dysfunctional, awful, do better if they can maintain rituals such as supper."[10]

No sense in going on about the magic of eating together. If you've experienced it pleasantly, you already get the point. If you haven't, you might consider taking more initiative in making happy meals happen, and we're not talking McDonald's. Could you offer to shop? To come home earlier? Pick up a younger sibling? Cook something? Set the table? Wake up a happily sleeping family member? Eat, without negative comment, something you're not crazy about? Play peacemaker at the table? Clean up?

If you have problems with family meals, it's probably worth trying to talk about them with adults in charge. Can the time of meals be changed? Can you have more input in choosing food? Can something be done to head off arguments, hassles, and/or moody silences? Can prep and cleanup be more fairly shared?

WHAT IF YOU CAN'T EAT WHAT THEY EAT?

Aside from not liking the taste of certain foods offered to you, you may have other objections or prohibitions. Let's say you're offered meat and potatoes and you want to be a vegetarian—or

Suzie Berkowitz has given up fast-food meat.

the other way around. Or the food-giver doesn't care about calories and you do. Of course, many parents are sensitive to kids' wishes, beliefs, and needs. They may even admire you for taking an opposing position.

But if differences stir up serious arguments, you may find yourself in a weak position—unless you're contributing to food costs. About one-third of teenagers work for money outside the home and yet only an estimated 3 percent contribute to family living expenses.[11] This statistic may change in times of economic stress. In any case, one way for a teen to gain a stronger voice in family food decisions is to put some money, or shared responsibility, into the family pot.

"I NEVER REALLY LIKED THE TASTE OF MEAT"

Let's say the problem isn't money. The problem is that you and your parents have a completely different take on what constitutes a reasonable diet. Let's say you're determined to be a vegetarian and your parents love meat. You're convinced that eating vegetarian is healthier, or more compassionate to animals, or better for global sustainability, or more in keeping

🍴 "MY MOM STILL ROLLS HER EYES"

Suzy Berkowitz, age seventeen, explains her sacrifice.

I had never thought of becoming a vegetarian. But after watching a video on slaughterhouses produced by PETA (People for the Ethical Treatment of Animals), I felt it would be an insult to every animal in the world to continue eating meat. For two weeks I was a closet vegetarian: not eating meat but not telling my mom about it.

She wouldn't understand. She grew up in a house full of carnivores, all of whom stressed the importance of a "red meat diet." My mom thinks no amount of vitamin supplements could ever match the nutrients meat provides.

I started eating salads for lunch and cooking myself spaghetti before my mom came home from work. The smell of turkey bacon one Saturday morning crept up my nose, tempting me like some sinful force. "No," I thought, starting at it. "I'm a vegetarian." It felt good to say it in my head.

After two weeks we went to a diner and my mom ordered me the chicken noodle soup. My heart raced. "How am I going to do this?" I looked at people sitting near me, casually munching on meat loaf or suckling at a chicken bone. "Those animals were tortured you know!" I felt like screaming.

The waiter placed the cup of soup in front of me. In it floated noodles and strips of gray meat. I could feel my mom's eyes on me. There was no way out. "I'm really sorry," I told the chicken.

That night at the diner was a reality check. It made me realize that as much as I would like to be a complete vegetarian, living with my mom makes it too hard for me. Then I thought about fast food and the things I'd seen in the movie *Super Size Me*. I decided that doing without fast food meat would be my contribution.

After a few weeks all I wanted was a McNugget. But when I stepped up to the counter, I took a deep breath and ordered fries. It was a big sacrifice to crave chicken but order something no animals had been killed to produce.

I haven't taken a bite of fast food meat for a year and a half now. My mom still rolls her eyes, and many of my friends still laugh when I order a salad instead of a sandwich. Some family members don't understand my sacrifice. I nod when they argue with me, but I never take their arguments into consideration. I consider my contribution something to be proud of simply because it's mine.

with religious beliefs, or all of the above, but your parents think you'll be jeopardizing your health—or that you've gone off your rocker. Your best defense will be showing evidence from books, articles, and websites, encouraging parents to talk to a doctor or nutritionist, and then proving your intentions by buying and preparing food and following a nutrition-rich vegetarian diet.

WHO'S A VEGETARIAN?[12]

A vegetarian is someone who never eats meat, poultry, fish, or other seafood. A vegan, in addition to rejecting meat, poultry, fish and seafood, never eats dairy products or eggs. In the United States, with a total population of over 300,000 million,

**more than 4 million adults claim to be vegetarians (about 2.3 percent);
more women are vegetarians than men; and
more people ages forty-five to fifty-four are vegetarians than people ages eighteen to twenty-four.**

A mostly happy vegetarian story is Victoria's.

I never really liked the taste of meat. If I ate in a restaurant I would try to order a dish without it. At home, I would feed most of it to my dog under the table.

. . . My father finally got tired of hearing me grumble about having to eat meat. . . . When I was twelve, he suggested that I become a vegetarian. Since he's a health nut, he pointed out that I had to balance my diet by eating more tofu and soybeans to make up for the lost protein. That wasn't a problem since I like both. My mother wasn't thrilled but she thought it was a phase I would soon get over.

After a few years of strains (some of her classmates thought that "all vegetarians were radical animal rights activist," and some of her relatives were strongly for, or strongly against, her position), Victoria reached the point of not feeling alone in her choice. She concludes, "I don't think I can ever go back and start eating meat again."[13]

AVOIDING FOODS WHEN YOU MUST

Becoming a vegetarian is a choice. Avoiding peanuts if you're allergic isn't. Let's hope that if you have a true food allergy, or even a food sensitivity, your family is aware of the condition and has already made adjustments. In fact, since food allergies tend to be inherited, chances are other members of your family have the same allergies or sensitivities as you do. Common ones are sensitivity to lactose (milk), sucrose (sugars), histamine

FOOD ALLERGIES[15]

What are food allergies?

A true food allergy is the reaction of the body's immune system to a food or food ingredient it recognizes as "foreign." A food intolerance, which typically affects the digestive system, is a bad reaction to a food, food ingredient, or additive that does *not* involve the immune system.

In true food allergies, what's happening in the body?

The immune system, while trying to fight a food "invader," releases powerful inflammatory chemicals that affect the body's own cells. True allergies and less serious sensitivities range from life threatening (anaphylactic shock) to mildly irritating.

What are common symptoms of food allergies and intolerances?

Food allergies often affect the skin, respiratory system, nervous system, and/or digestive tract. Specific symptoms include fever, chills, aches, rashes, swelling, itching, sneezing, coughing, labored breathing, headache, nausea, vomiting, diarrhea, indigestion, and sweating.

How many people have food allergies and who is vulnerable?

Between 5 and 8 percent of children are estimated to have true food allergies. These usually decrease over time, down to 1–2 percent in adulthood. Food intolerances, often minor and hard to test for, are so common that almost everyone has had an experience. (Food poisoning, caused by toxic food, is not the same as food allergy.) Research hasn't yet made clear why only some people are allergic, but the answer seems to be linked to genetics, history since birth, and lifestyle.

(aged cheeses, processed meats, etc.), salicylate (certain salts), and artificial food color, preservatives, monosodium glutamate, and nuts. Because most food allergies are acquired during the first year of life,[14] you're probably not going to be shocked by the appearance of a true allergy at this point.

Discovering the cause of a food sensitivity isn't that easy. First, because you typically eat more than one thing at a time, it's hard to pinpoint the offending substance. Second, depending on its freshness and origin, the same food may cause you to react differently at different times. And third, the exact condition of your body at the time of eating may leave you more, or less, vulnerable to a problem food. Allergists—that is, specialists in the area of tracking down causes of allergies and intolerances—use, among other means, skin tests, blood tests, and patch tests to do their detective work. The trouble is that these tests sometimes give false-positive or false-negative results. That's why experts agree that "for the most accurate results, a detailed medical history, family history, and physical exam should always accompany testing."[16]

Allergy testing results are frequently surprising and unclear. For instance, because sensitivity to peanuts affects up to 1.5 million people per year in the United States, doctors have often recommended that small children and nursing mothers refrain from eating them. A recent study, however, indicates that babies of nine months who had already been exposed to peanuts were six times *less* likely to develop an allergy to them.[17]

"One Bite Can Be Deadly"

Even though most allergic reactions are annoying more than life threatening, about 150 Americans per year die from anaphylactic reactions to food. Among deaths studied, researchers found that most victims were teenagers or young adults; most were eating away from home; most failed to get, or to pay attention to, ingredient information; and more than 80 percent were reacting to peanuts or tree nuts (almonds, cashews, or pecans).[18] These tragedies hardly ever occur out of the blue. Typically, a young person, perhaps one who's asthmatic and also aware of a serious allergy, becomes careless

🍴 "I ALWAYS CARRY MY EPIPEN"

Anne, age nineteen, talks about her lifelong allergies.

I have a life-threatening allergy to peanuts, nuts, legumes, and soy. I discovered my allergy when I was one year old. My mom gave me a typical childhood lunch—peanut butter and jelly. Within seconds my face became swollen and I stopped breathing. After being rushed to the hospital, we found out about my allergy. I was then tested and we discovered my other food allergies.

I am still highly allergic to peanuts, nuts, and soy. I had an allergic reaction to sprinkles at an ice cream shop once when I was younger, but I take really good care of myself, always carry my EpiPen, and read ingredients on all items I eat.

I used to consider my allergies as a nuisance, but as I get older I realize that it is not that big a problem. I am in control of my allergy and could never let it control me.

about checking ingredients and accidentally eats the wrong thing. If he or she has been trained to carry self-injecting epinephrine, a crisis can be averted, but without the right medication—administered quickly—the mistake can be fatal.[19]

Since 2006 a universal symbol has been available to call attention to kids' allergies. Colorado mom Robyn O'Brien created

Anne Gole has learned to control her allergies instead of letting them control her.

a green-stop-sign-plus-exclamation-point design, found on stickers and charms, intended to be attached to kids' lunch boxes and clothes. O'Brien, who became an activist when her youngest child had a bad reaction to scrambled eggs, has appeared on news programs and has established a website, AllergyKids.com.[20]

Being Your Brother's or Sister's Keeper

If you yourself have ever had a life-threatening reaction to food, you have probably learned by now to be cautious and prepared. But maybe you haven't given much thought to the sensitivities of relatives and friends. Let's say your sibling can't eat peanuts or a friend is allergic to shrimp. You'll be doing them a big favor, when eating in their company, to remind them to check ingredients. For some processed foods the total ingredient list goes on forever. Fortunately, though, since 2004 the Food and Drug Administration has required producers to say, in plain English, whether the product contains any of the eight most common causes of allergic reactions—milk, eggs, fish, shellfish, tree nuts, peanuts, wheat, and soybeans.[21]

Whether it's you or someone you're with who is vulnerable to food allergies, remember prevention, prevention, prevention. The allergic person (and you) should spread the word about the allergy, so that unsuspecting food givers don't offer problematical foods. Allergic persons should study ingredient lists, bring their own food when necessary, wear medical alert bracelets, carry EpiPens (devices to inject epinephrine), and develop an action plan for what's to be done in an anaphylactic emergency.[22]

Regardless of how large or small your family is, and how often or rarely you eat together, somebody, sometime in your family has to bring food home and get it to the table. If you aren't that person now, you probably will be someday. Read on.

NOTES

1. "The 5 Benefits—and a Few Risks—of Eating Together at the Dinner Table," 1, Sixwise.com, www.sixwise.com/newsletters/06/05/03/the_5_benefits_--_and_a_few_risks_--_of_eating_together_at_the_dinner_table.htm (accessed October 28, 2008).

2. Suzanna Smith, "Are Families Dining Together?" University of Florida IFAS, fycs.ifas.ufl.edu/newsletters/rnycu06/2006/01/are-families-dining-together.html (accessed October 28, 2008).

3. "Eating Together as a Family Creates Better Eating Habits Later in Life," *ScienceDaily*, September 4, 2007, 1 www.sciencedaily.com/releases/2007/09/070901073612.htm (accessed October 6, 2008).

4. Nancy Gibbs, "The Magic of the Family Meal," *Time*, June 4, 2006, 2, www.time.com/magazine/article/0,9171,1200760,00.html (accessed October 6, 2008).

5. Gibbs, "The Magic of the Family Meal," 2.

6. Tara Parker-Pope, "The Family Meal Is What Counts, TV On or Off," *New York Times*, October 16, 2007, F5.

7. "The 5 Benefits—and a Few Risks—of Eating Together at the Dinner Table," 1.

8. Tara Parker-Pope, "Guess Who's Coming to Dinner: Your Teen," *New York Times* blog, October 17, 2007, well.blogs.nytimes.com/2007/10/17/guess-whos-coming-to-dinner-your-teen/ (accessed February 19, 2009).

9. "Out of the Mouth of Teenagers," October 13, 2008, fabulousfinancials.com/2008/10/out-the-mouth-of-teenagers.html (accessed October 23, 2008).

10. Miriam Weinstein, *The Surprising Power of Family Meals* (Hanover, NH: Steerforth Press, 2005), 12.

11. Charles Stahle, "How Many Adults Are Vegetarian?" *Vegetarian Journal*, no. 4 (2006), www.vrg.org/journal/vj2006issue4/vj2006issue4poll.htm (accessed March 5, 2008).

12. "Teenagers: Employment and Money Management," Adoption.com, library.adoption.com/articles/teenagers-employment-and-money-management.html (accessed November 4, 2008).

13. Victoria Law, "Becoming a Vegetarian: A Matter of Taste," in *Starting with I: Personal Essays by Teenagers*, ed. Andrea Estepa and Philip Kay (New York: Persea Books, 1997), 137–40.

14. Vesanto Melina, Jo Stepaniak, and Dina Aronson, *Food Allergy Survival Guide* (Summertown, TN: Healthy Living Publications, 2004), 13–15.

15. Melina, Stepaniak, and Aronson, *Food Allergy Survival Guide*, 8–12

16. Melina, Stepaniak, and Aronson, *Food Allergy Survival Guide*, 65–68.

17. Anahad Conner, "Really?" *New York Times*, November 25, 2008, D5.

18. Sharona Schwartz, "Food Allergies: One Bite Can Be Deadly," CNN.com, March 27, 2007, 1, www.cnn.com/2007/HEALTH/conditions/03/26/food.allergies/index.html (accessed November 5, 2008).

19. Schwartz, "Food Allergies," 2.

20. Kim Severson, "Food Allergies Stir a Mother to Action," *New York Times*, January 9, 2008, F1, F8.

21. Marion Nestle, *What to Eat* (New York: North Point Press, 2006), 279.

22. Melina, Stepaniak, and Aronson, *Food Allergy Survival Guide*, 124–25.

6 Bringing Food Home

How much input do you have when it comes to food shopping? Whether it's just you and one other person, or ten people every night at dinner, someone's got to buy food and lug it home—or order in.

As you might guess, "the vast majority of women (85%) say they do most of the grocery shopping for their families," a percentage that has stayed about the same since 1998. Lately, though, men claim to be shopping more often for food, suggesting that "more men perceive that they're helping out . . . even though most women still believe they're doing the lion's share."[1] Figuring on the basis of time per day, women spend 8.4 minutes, on average, shopping for food as opposed to 4.2 minutes for men.[2]

In some cases, of course, family members take turns or shop together. Teenagers supposedly spend billions of dollars a year on groceries, but how much of it is their own money remains unclear.[3]

TO MARKET, TO MARKET . . .

If you grew up riding inside a supermarket cart and are now the cart pusher, you may already know an organic label from a "loss leader." But if you don't shop for food on a regular basis, this chapter is one place to begin. How do you decide what to buy, how much to buy, and where to buy it? How do you know what tastes good, and how do you get the best price? Even if you don't need to know all this now, you probably will someday soon.

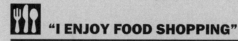

"I ENJOY FOOD SHOPPING"

Eimarc Reyes, age seventeen, doesn't mind going to the supermarket.

When my mother can't go shopping, I go, usually with my little brother and sister, who are seven and six. My mother and father give me the money, and I enjoy food shopping, especially when I take my siblings. Mostly we buy fruit and vegetables; meat; drinks like milk, juice, and soda; and cans of corn and beans.

Our favorite fruits include strawberries, watermelon, cherries, apples, oranges, and kiwis, and the most common vegetables we buy are lettuce, tomatoes, celery, and carrots. Some produce is expensive; cherries, for instance. That's bad, because many cherries are ruined and go into the garbage. The owner should lower the price a little, so people buy them and they don't go to waste.

There are times when my little brother and sister just want me to buy junk food: big bags of chips, soda, cookies, and candy. Sometimes I just buy one item and give them only one piece at a time. For example, when I buy them cookies I give them three cookies each with a cup of milk.

Eimarc Reyes does a supermarket shop for her family when her mother can't go.

CHOICES

In contrast to your caveman ancestors, who went out and killed or picked something edible, in the twenty-first century you've got access to a range of choices—from huge supermarkets and discount stores, to specialized chains, to farmers' markets, to online ordering. If you're not yet involved in serious food shopping, someday soon you'll have to make food-buying decisions that will probably depend on quality, price, variety, and convenience.

Are you already tuned in to the following? You're probably going to have to pay more for convenience. If wide choice is important to you, you'll probably have to shop at more than one market. If top quality is your highest priority, you'll be paying top dollar. And if saving money comes first, you'll need to clip coupons, read ads, make lists, check the Internet, read labels, buy in bulk, buy imperfect items, and reuse bags.

WHERE TO SHOP FOR FOOD—BESIDES SUPERMARKETS

Walmart or other superstores. Alternatives to big supermarkets are even bigger supermarkets, where you and your family can save money on food. An independent study showed that shoppers who spent $100 per week on groceries could save an average of $700 per year by buying similar groceries at Walmart.[4]

Thrift stores, wholesale outlets, and dollar stores. Want some day-old bread? Sometimes thrift stores specialize in the products of one manufacturer (of baked goods, for instance), and sometimes they're more general. In any case, purchases made here may be cheaper because goods are outdated, containers imperfect, or items discontinued. But food is generally acceptable, and with careful examination you can get great buys. Most dollar stores also sell no-frills, no-fancy-label edibles.

IGAs. IGA, which stands for Independent Grocery Alliance, is an organization of nearly 4,000 so-called Hometown Proud small supermarkets in forty-four states and forty countries. This alliance allows separately run stores to get some of the benefits of a big operation without having to cave in to decisions made by out-of-town executives.[5]

(continued)

WHERE TO SHOP FOR FOOD—BESIDES SUPERMARKETS *(Continued)*

Specialty and premium food shops. Are you looking for Italian sausages, bagels, or fresh Chinese vegetables? Specialty food stores, such as bakeries, delicatessens, and ethnic groceries, have existed for years in America, mostly in cities but even in small towns. A more recent development is the gourmet specialty food shop or chain (like Whole Foods, started about 1980).

Farm stands, farmers markets, and street vendors. Have you ever gone out to pick apples, berries, or pumpkins? Farmers selling food directly to customers is another longtime tradition. In season, farmers and their workers often operate road stands and/or offer customers the chance to pick produce themselves. Growers also bring produce into cities and towns, where shoppers expect to find freshness and a selection of organic foods. Quality in farmers' markets usually surpasses that of supermarkets, and even though prices may be higher, good buys are likely, in season.

Once-a-week farmers' markets are doing well these days, patronized by about a quarter million shoppers a year in New York City alone.[6] Lately these markets are being made available to a wider range of people, including low-income customers using federally funded vouchers.[7]

Food cooperatives (co-ops). Does your family have access to a co-op—a cooperative grocery or produce-selling arrangement? Such groups, which started in England in the 1840s, took hold in the United States in the 1970s and are popular today. For an agreed-upon amount of money, your family would be entitled, weekly or monthly, to a certain amount of goods—usually including fresh produce. Some people join co-ops to save money, but others care more about gaining more control over food quality and gaining satisfaction from supporting local farmers

---

THE RISE OF THE SUPERMARKET

Your great- or great-great-grandparents, used to slow eating, were probably also used to slow shopping. At a local market they waited for a butcher to cut meat to order and a grocer to measure out butter or flour. Food shopping began to change when the first self-service grocery store, Piggly Wiggly, opened in Memphis, Tennessee, in 1916 and when the first true U.S. supermarket, King Kullen, opened in Queens, New York City, in 1930.[8]

After World War II there was no stopping the spread of supermarkets. Farmlands were replaced by housing developments, more families could afford automobiles, and refrigerators and freezers appeared in most kitchens. Everywhere in America, but especially in the suburbs, shoppers came to appreciate the supermarket's wide selection of foods and household products, plus convenient parking and shopping hours.

Supermarkets Now

How many supermarkets are within a mile or two of your neighborhood? At this point about 40 percent of all U.S. food purchases are made from supermarkets, to the tune of $350 billion a year. In any one store you'll find about 40,000 items.[9] But even though supermarkets are well established and can, as part of a chain, afford to sell at lower prices, these days they're in a decline. Shoppers are shopping less often and spending less money. A lot of competitors have been challenging supermarkets, so that, for instance, "in 2001, Wal-Mart became the largest seller of food."[10] As a result of this competition, the supermarket industry is trying new ideas to win customers away from not only superstores but also from gourmet boutiques, dollar stores, and online ordering.

How Do They Draw Us In?

Take a trip to your nearest supermarket. See that sushi? That ATM machine? Those bins of organic produce? That speedy self-service checkout? Those are some of the innovations they're trying to lure more shoppers in. Notice the array of prepared foods, which shouldn't surprise us, since estimates indicate that 40 percent of people don't know what they're having for dinner at 4:00 P.M. the same day.[11]

Does your market have a "meal deal"—that is, a coupon for a balanced family dinner for four, complete with choices and nutrition facts, all for a modest price? Are they handing out flyers with money-saving tips, recipes, and nutritional information? Do they have a website where you can go for prices and coupons?

WHAT'S YOUR SUPERMARKET IQ?[12]

How come freshly baked bread is usually put at the entrance to the supermarket?

Supermarkets hope the smell of freshly baked bread and the sight of flowers will put you in a buying mood. They think you may buy, on impulse, items located up front.

Why is it that you usually have to trek to the back of the store for something basic, like a container of milk?

Chances are you'll have to go back to where the basics are located. On the way you may pick up items you didn't intend to buy.

What's the purpose of those annoying little stickers on each piece of fresh fruit?

Those stickers indicate either that the item is organically grown or grown in a particular location.

Supermarkets feature a few products each week—usually juice, or a certain brand of coffee, or an item of fresh produce— that they refer to as "loss leaders." What does the term mean?

Loss leaders are basic items offered below cost in order to lure you into the store on the assumption that you'll buy other things while you're there.

How come apples, cucumbers, and such are often coated with wax?

Fresh produce is often coated with a harmless (fatty) wax that replaces lost natural waxes. Wax protects produce from mold and bruising, makes it look fresher, and enables it to last longer on the shelf. "Waxes are a nuisance, not a health problem."

Probably your market is trying to save you time by offering catering and other services such as on-site dry cleaning. Supermarkets are also experimenting with computer technology, so that they can analyze your individual buying habits. When you check out, you may receive a coupon for an item that corresponds to one on your current receipt. In other words, the computer knows what you like and is nudging you toward buying it again.

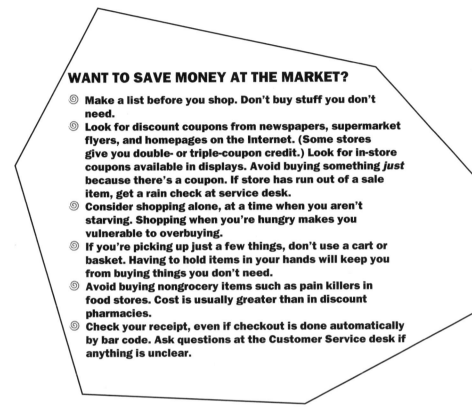

WANT TO SAVE MONEY AT THE MARKET?

◎ **Make a list before you shop. Don't buy stuff you don't need.**

◎ **Look for discount coupons from newspapers, supermarket flyers, and homepages on the Internet. (Some stores give you double- or triple-coupon credit.) Look for in-store coupons available in displays. Avoid buying something *just* because there's a coupon. If store has run out of a sale item, get a rain check at service desk.**

◎ **Consider shopping alone, at a time when you aren't starving. Shopping when you're hungry makes you vulnerable to overbuying.**

◎ **If you're picking up just a few things, don't use a cart or basket. Having to hold items in your hands will keep you from buying things you don't need.**

◎ **Avoid buying nongrocery items such as pain killers in food stores. Cost is usually greater than in discount pharmacies.**

◎ **Check your receipt, even if checkout is done automatically by bar code. Ask questions at the Customer Service desk if anything is unclear.**

Anything Wrong with Supermarkets?

Especially if you aren't a regular customer, you may find supermarkets overwhelming and impersonal. Some shoppers fault them for their limited selection of fresh produce. Another gripe is that so-called fresh produce may have come from far away, been picked unripe, and doctored in some way to make it look fresh. Another negative is that supermarkets, with their variety and low prices, drive out smaller, local, family-owned stores.

In spite of criticisms, supermarkets aren't going to disappear. According to writer David Kamp, "Slowly but surely the supermarket is transforming itself from a lowest-common-denominator vendor of pale iceberg lettuce and Spam into a hybrid store that sells both the prepackaged, processed stuff that America will always have an appetite for *and* the fresher, healthier, better-tasting stuff that the premium markets sell."[13]

TELEPHONE AND ONLINE ORDERING

Let's say you and your family hate to go food shopping. You avoid it by ordering out for pizza or Chinese food. As you may know, you can avoid supermarkets altogether by ordering, by phone or online, all your groceries from home. Some local stores offer you the possibility of choosing from thousands of online selections, in which case a local employee, working from a printout, will fill your order and arrange delivery. Other companies, operating from large central warehouses, ship orders from a distance. Of course, you'll be paying extra for extra service.

GROWING YOUR OWN PRODUCE

If you decide to grow some of your own food, you'll have plenty of company. One quarter of all households grow some of their own produce, according to the U.S. Census Bureau.[14] Companies that sell seeds, plants, and gardening equipment report that business hasn't been as good since the inflationary 1970s, and those who want plots in community gardens often have to put their names on waiting lists these days.[15]

"I'm currently working on a garden but having a bit of trouble staying dedicated. My grandpa always worked on his garden and had quite a few fruit trees, figs in particular. My mom and I also have a fig tree in the backyard and a compost bin for the garden. Growing a garden is fun but often frustrating. Next summer I am definitely going to try to grow a lot more of my own food."
—Alex, age fifteen

Well-known writer Barbara Kingsolver overcame major frustrations to prove that she and her family could be truly food self-sufficient. They left a conventional life in Arizona for a farm in Virginia, where they lived for a year exclusively on food they raised themselves, plus some that was grown in their neighborhood.

Let's say you like the idea of gardening but don't feel like making all that effort. If you happen to live in San Francisco

106

🍴 "MY PLAN IS TO HAVE MY OWN FARM SOMEDAY"

Tim Smith, age nineteen, is a summer worker at Pike's Farm in Sagaponack, New York, and says the following about farming:

My usual responsibilities on the farm are planting most of the plants, hoeing and weeding, assembling tractor equipment, setting irrigation pipes, putting up fences, and picking produce.

If a friend asked me what my job was like, I would say, "It can be trying at times and it can drain you, but the pay ain't bad, and I am doing what I want to do and I enjoy it." I'm blessed with the job I have. Being able to work outside and do the things that I want to do are obviously beneficial. I got this job because my plan is to have my own farm one day. I need to learn somewhere.

Tim Smith is working part time now, but he'd like to own his own farm someday.

and have enough money—no problem. You can hire Trevor Paque, a gardener-for-hire, who will set up a garden on your property, weed it, and leave the results on your doorstep.[16]

Or, at the other end of the spectrum, if you love working the land, you can prepare, like Tim Smith, age nineteen, to make farming your occupation.

DO YOU KNOW ANY "FREEGANS"?

Or let's say you can't bear the thought of wasted food and you really like saving money. Freegans, many of whom are vegans, are people willing to dive into food-market Dumpsters in search of free meals. Although this alternative food-gathering method may sound more like a teenage dare than a viable option, adults, like Madeline Nelson who was once a bookstore director, routinely get most of what they eat from trash just before it's carted off to the dump. Freegans are usually motivated more by politics than poverty. They don't like supporting businesses that waste resources and harm the environment. In addition to plucking salad and carrots out of Whole Foods Dumpsters, Nelson looks for discarded prepared foods and freezes day-old baked goods that have been tossed.[17]

IF THERE ISN'T ENOUGH MONEY FOR FOOD

Most of us can't afford private gardeners. Many families struggle to put enough food on the table. And in certain times and places, no matter how many food bargains are out there, people would go hungry without getting help. In the world, an estimated 923 million go hungry. In the United States, 11.7 million children live in households where meals have to be skipped.[18]

Help for hungry people usually comes in one of two ways—from governments or from religious or other charitable organizations. In the United States, off and on since 1939, the federal government has offered assistance through a program once called the Food Stamp Program and now called SNAP (Supplemental Nutrition Assistance Program). SNAP helps those in low-income households to get adequate nutrition. Even though the program as a whole is federal, individual SNAPs are administered by states. These days, instead of stamps, qualified recipients get special ATM cards to be used in stores for food-only purchases. Use of the cards is restricted—for instance, no pre-cooked foods, no toothpaste, no beer or cigarettes.

WHO IS ELIGIBLE FOR SNAP?

Eligibility varies from state to state and generally depends on a family's income, the number and age of family members, and their citizenship status. In 2008 about 10 percent of the U.S. population was receiving SNAP benefits, which averaged out to about $100 per month per family member.[19] Those who believe they're eligible can apply at a local SNAP office or get an application on the Internet.

FOOD BANKS, PANTRIES, AND SOUP KITCHENS

Let's say a family's SNAP credit has run out for the month and they're still hungry. Religious, community, and government groups often set up nonprofit food pantries for emergencies and tough times. More than 200 food banks in a network called America's Second Harvest get supplies from private donations, items donated by companies and supermarkets, and from U.S. Department of Agriculture farm surplus stock. Some pantries serve only a few families a month and others serve hundreds— or more, at holiday time.[20]

In times of economic stress the demand for food can be so great that pantries, like one recently in Winston-Salem, North Carolina, have to turn hungry people away. In North Carolina, food-bank director Kitty Schaller is worried about the 330 pantries she supplies, because expenses are going up and donations are going down.[21] Bill Bolling, director of the Atlanta Community Food Bank in Georgia, reported in 2008 that he had never seen anything like the current situation, in which people who were once donors now needed help themselves.[22]

If you happen to be looking for a place to volunteer your services, a nearby food bank or soup kitchen may need your help.

MEALS ON WHEELS

Maybe you know someone—a grandparent—who needs the help of a food bank but can't there because of ill health. For the homebound there's a safety net known as Meals on Wheels. This organization, founded in Great Britain and operating in the United States since 1954, is paid for by a combination of government and private donations. The meals, consisting of hot food, microwaveable cold food, and frozen foods, are delivered daily to those who would otherwise go hungry.[23]

Bringing home the bacon, for some families, is a pleasant trip to a market or a quick call for takeout. Other families struggle to find food bargains or resign themselves to waiting in line for free food. If you're in the lucky majority, you'll have a lifetime food choices, and the biggest struggle you'll face will be how to decide.

NOTES

1. "Who's Really Doing the Grocery Shopping? (Consumer Spending & Attitudes)," Access My Library, www.accessmylibrary.com/coms2/summary_0286-2928052_ITM (accessed November 12, 2008).

2. Karen Hamrick and Kristina Shelley, "How Much Time Do Americans Spend Preparing and Eating Food?" *Amber Waves*, November 2005, www.ers.usda.gov/AmberWaves/November05/DataFeature/ (accessed November 12, 2008).

3. "When Teens Take Over the Shopping Cart," U.S. Food and Drug Administration, March 1990, www.fda.gov/bbs/topics/CONSUMER/CON00078.html (accessed November 12, 2008).

4. "Shoppers Spending $100 a Week Could Save an Average of $700 a Year on Similar Packaged Groceries at Walmart," http://walmartstores.com/FactsNews/NewsRoom/8594.aspx (accessed January 20, 2010).

5. "About IGA," IGA, www.iga.com/aboutIGA/about.aspx (accessed November 20, 2008).

6. Barbara Kingsolver, *Animal, Vegetable, Miracle* (New York: HarperCollins, 2007), 20.

7. Tara Parker-Pope, "The Farmers' Market Effect," *New York Times* blog, January 15, 2008, well.blogs.nytimes.com/2008/01/15/the-farmers-market-effect/?emc=etal (accessed November 22, 2008).

8. "Supermarket," Wikipedia, 2, en.wikipedia.org/wiki/Supermarket (accessed November 13, 2008).

9. Marion Nestle, *What to Eat* (New York: North Point Press, 2006), 33, 17.

10. Thom Imlay, "Challenges in Today's U.S. Supermarket Industry," MSDN, May 2006, 1, msdn.microsoft.com/en-us/library/aa479076(printer).aspx (accessed November 19, 2008).

11. Nestle, *What to Eat*, 17–21.

12. Imlay, "Challenges in Today's U.S. Supermarket Industry," 2.

13. David Kamp, *The United States of Arugula* (New York: Broadway Books, 2006), 360.

14. Kingsolver, *Animal, Vegetable, Miracle*, 20.

15. Marian Burros, "Banking on Gardening," *New York Times*, June 11, 2008, www.nytimes.com/2008/06/11/dining/11garden.html?n=Top/Reference/Times%20 (accessed November 20, 2008).

16. Kim Severson, "A Locally Grown Diet with Fuss but No Muss," *New York Times*, July 22, 2008, 1–2, www.nytimes.com/2008/07/22/dining/22local.html?em (accessed November 25, 2008).

17. "People Who Can Afford Food Forage Instead, and Like It," from *Los Angeles Times* in *Reading Eagle*, September 14, 2007, A7.

18. "Hunger Facts," Bread for the World, www.bread.org/learn/hunger-basics/ (accessed December 4, 2008).

19. "Food Stamp Program," Wikipedia, en.wikipedia.org/wiki/Food_Stamp_Program (accessed December 5, 2008).

20. "Food Bank," Wikipedia, en.wikipedia.org/wiki/Food_bank (accessed December 4, 2008).

21. David Cay Johnston, "When the Cupboard Is Bare," *New York Times*, November 10, 2008, www.nytimes.com/2008/11/11/giving/11FOOD.html?_r=1 (accessed December 9, 2008).

22. Katie Zezima, "From Canned Goods to Fresh, Food Banks Adapt to Demand," *New York Times*, December 10, 2008, A1.

23. "Meals on Wheels," Wikipedia, en.wikipedia.org/wiki/Meals_on_Wheels (accessed December 9, 2008).

7 | How Safe Is the Food You Eat?

You come back from a ball game and don't feel so good. Could it have been the hot dog? You come home from a picnic and feel *really* bad. Later you find out other kids got sick, too. Most people, at some point, get sick from something they ate. Usually the effect is mild and goes away quickly. Sometimes the result is serious.

First, let's get past the bad news. Every year about 76 million Americans suffer a food-borne illness. Of those, about 325,000 have to go to a hospital, and—here comes the unthinkable— 5,000 die.[1] If these statistics make it seem as if starvation is less risky, think about the billions of people daily who eat without suffering the slightest twinge. Still, that thought isn't much comfort to families of victims of salmonella or E. coli poisoning.

WHAT IS FOOD POISONING?

Food poisoning is a bad reaction to food, caused either by an infectious agent (a virus, or bacteria, or parasite), or a toxic agent (found in poisonous mushrooms or in strong pesticides). How do you know if you've got food poisoning? Symptoms, from mild to life threatening, include nausea, vomiting, abdominal cramps, diarrhea, chills and fever, headache, and weakness.

The most serious forms of food poisoning are salmonella, E. coli, Listeria, and botulism. Bad effects are usually felt within a couple of hours of eating the problem food, but botulism symptoms may not surface for as long as twelve to thirty-six hours. Food poisoning is relatively rare in the United States, but in the rest of the world between 60 and 80 million people each year are affected and 6 to 8 million people die.[2]

Which Foods Cause the Most Problems?

You've been told forever to wash fruit before you eat it. Even though any edibles can become contaminated if they're mishandled—by farmers, packers, or people in your own house—foods at highest risk of contamination are red meats and poultry, raw fish and shell fish, eggs, dairy products (including cheese), and raw sprouts. Some foods are vulnerable to bacteria and parasites right at the source. For instance, cases of E. coli have been traced to spinach and lettuce grown in fields polluted with the runoff from cow manure. Generally speaking, produce that grows close to the ground is more likely to be tainted.

You've also probably been told not to eat salad dressing or cake batter that contains raw eggs. That's because each year in the United States egg yolks, along with raw and undercooked poultry, dairy products, fish, and seafood, may cause as many as 50,000 cases of salmonella. According to the Centers for Disease Control and Prevention your chances are one-in-fifty each year of being exposed to a contaminated egg.[3]

Besides that, contamination can occur during the packing process. E. coli has been found in beef, and the illness Listeria has been traced to hot dogs. Botulism may occur in foods that haven't been canned properly. And finally, foods that aren't refrigerated well enough, or are kept too long, may go bad. That's why you and your family should be especially careful if you leave food outdoors over a period of a few hours. When you're a guest it's tricky to check on other people's standards, but be wary of street food, food from a salad bar, or lunch you carry in hot weather.

The main point is, if you suspect you have, or someone you know has, food poisoning, take action. If the symptoms are severe, or if symptoms last more than two days, call or see a doctor, or go to an emergency room.

🍴 "I BECAME OVERWHELMED"

Elizabeth Acton, now in her early twenties, suffered from food poisoning as a teenager.

I first experienced food poisoning when I was fourteen. For a special treat our family had ordered Chinese food. I liked egg drop soup and ordered it when we had Chinese. No more than fifteen minutes after eating this viscous egg mixture I became overwhelmed with nausea, hot, and light-headed. I spent the entire evening vomiting. I tried to drink as much water as possible, hoping to flush out the awful feeling. Now at the very sight or scent of egg drop soup I cringe uncontrollably.

My second and perhaps worse experience with food poisoning came two years later from a packet of tuna. Instead of canned tuna, some brands had come out with packets, very easy to use to make tuna salad. Again, as with the egg drop soup, it took no more than fifteen minutes to realize I was experiencing the onset of food poisoning. Like the first time, I became overwhelmed with nausea. This time, however, I could not keep anything down for nearly two days and was nauseous at the very idea of food. Since then I have yet to eat, or stomach being in the presence of, canned tuna. The smell turns my stomach, and this was some years ago.

By the way, the food poisoning I experienced wasn't from adventurous food trials but from food I was comfortable with until the incidents.

WORST SCENARIOS

In recent years food-poisoning outbreaks have received so much media attention that some eaters have become paranoid and all of us wonder what's next. A number of tourists, in separate incidents, have gotten sick on cruise ships. Closer to home, in 2007 salmonella sickened almost 400 people who ate popular brands of peanut butter.[4] And a million and a half pounds of tainted ground beef was recalled in the mid-2000s, including 37 million pounds that went to school lunch programs.[5]

WHY SO MUCH FOOD-BORNE ILLNESS?

First, some food contamination occurs on farms, when manure pollutes water. Second, even more contamination occurs when produce is pre-bagged or when food is sold "prepared." The point is, the greater the number of workers involved in processing foods, the greater the chance of the spread of pathogens by unhealthy workers.[6] So, even though washing farm-fresh salad greens may take a little extra time, those greens are likely to be safer than pre-washed, bagged salad.

Food safety also becomes a greater problem when foods are imported from other countries—countries that may have lower standards than the United States for growing and processing food.

Amazing, isn't it, that most of us consume three meals a day and rarely get sick from what we eat?

WHO'S LOOKING OUT FOR YOUR HEALTH?

At least three groups are, or ought to be, responsible for your food safety.

1. **Farmers and producers themselves. It's good business for them to keep you well.**
2. **Agencies of the government, especially the Food and Drug Administration (FDA), an agency of the U.S. Department of Health and Human Services. They're elected, appointed, and hired to keep us safe.**
3. **Private watchdog groups, your family, and yourself. Citizens need to check on producers and agencies to make sure they're doing their jobs.**

One private citizen, Elizabeth Armstrong, is an example of an ordinary citizen who became a food safety activist. She had a very personal reason as the mother of a two-year-old daughter affected by E. coli in spinach.[7]

The FDA

Some say the main organization looking out for your health has an impossible job. The FDA is responsible not only for safety in 65,000 food-producing firms around the country, but also for safety of imported food and nonfood items, including drugs, vaccines, veterinary products, and cosmetics. It's responsible for setting standards and then conducting inspections to make sure that standards are met.

And, as if *that* wasn't enough to deal with, the FDA is also in charge of enforcing health regulations, from big stuff down to disease in pet turtles.[8] Given the enormity of their job, it's almost understandable that the FDA could miss something— and they have. Five federal inspectors at the California's Westland/Hallmark failed to detect that diseased cows were slaughtered for hamburger. As already mentioned, some of that hamburger ended up in school lunches.[9] That school could have been yours.

How Are Mistakes Made?

Health crises have sometimes been caused by human error—ignorance, carelessness, or FDA favoritism shown to food producers. Other safety problems have come about because of poor collaboration among the twelve agencies that are supposed to share responsibility. In still other cases, the FDA was on the job but health officials in other countries didn't cooperate. And, finally, certain oversights might have been avoided if the FDA had been given a bigger budget.

As you read this, the FDA claims to be making improvements in its approach to food inspection. Imported foods are supposedly going to be monitored more carefully in the future. New FDA offices in China, India, Europe, Latin America, and the Middle East will be focusing on detecting contamination before products enter the United States. The FDA is also committed to hiring more employees, giving extra attention to the inspection of high-risk domestic food establishments, and using irradiation to kill bacteria on leafy produce.[10]

Anything You Can Do?

You can try to protect yourself and your family by buying food carefully and storing it properly. You can report health

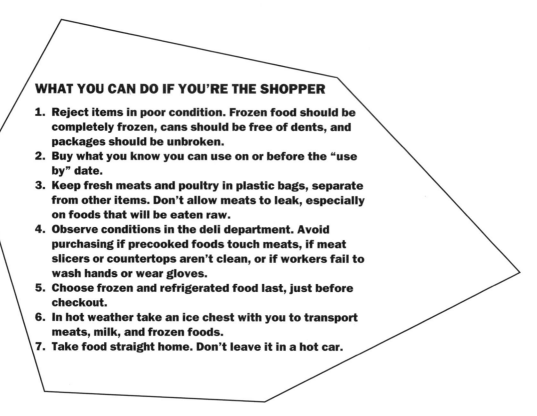

WHAT YOU CAN DO IF YOU'RE THE SHOPPER

1. Reject items in poor condition. Frozen food should be completely frozen, cans should be free of dents, and packages should be unbroken.
2. Buy what you know you can use on or before the "use by" date.
3. Keep fresh meats and poultry in plastic bags, separate from other items. Don't allow meats to leak, especially on foods that will be eaten raw.
4. Observe conditions in the deli department. Avoid purchasing if precooked foods touch meats, if meat slicers or countertops aren't clean, or if workers fail to wash hands or wear gloves.
5. Choose frozen and refrigerated food last, just before checkout.
6. In hot weather take an ice chest with you to transport meats, milk, and frozen foods.
7. Take food straight home. Don't leave it in a hot car.

threats or bad outcomes to market managers or to local health inspectors. High school student Leonard Chung went one step further by writing a piece for his local newspaper in which he criticized the USDA's (U.S. Department of Agriculture) lax standards in inspecting beef for export.[11]

OBAMA AND FOOD SAFETY

One of President Barack Obama's first acts after taking office was to create the Food Safety Working Group to advise him on which laws and regulations need to be changed. "In the end," says President Obama, "food safety is something I take seriously, not just as your president, but as a parent."[12]

A CONTROVERSIAL SAFETY PROCESS

In this advanced age, how come a kid can be laid low from food poisoning? We go to the moon. We transplant hearts. Can't we zap food to make it safe? Yes, we can, but not everybody likes the idea of irradiation. Irradiation is the process of using low amounts of X-rays to kill bacteria in foods such as grains, fruits, vegetables, and meats. Even though it was originally approved by the FDA back in 1963, many individuals and organizations object to its use. Those in favor of irradiation, such as the FDA and the American Medical Association, say that although irradiation doesn't kill all bacteria, the process makes food safer and doesn't affect nutrition.

Opponents, such as an organization called Food & Water Watch, claim that irradiation is expensive, not completely effective, ruinous to flavor and texture of food, and possibly, in the long run, dangerous to health. The American public has so far been skeptical about irradiated foods, which are required to be labeled and marked with a radura symbol.[13]

ORGANIC FOODS

What else can you do to improve your chances of eating safely? Well, for one thing, if you grow produce yourself, or consistently buy food labeled organic, you'll know that you aren't consuming harmful pesticides. The trouble is that even at a farm stand, produce may or may not be organic. Exactly how is the term defined, and how do you know for sure what's organic?

U.S. government standards define organic as foods grown "without the use of conventional pesticides and artificial fertilizers, free from contamination by human or industrial waste, and processed without ionizing radiation or food additives." Organic livestock must be raised without using antibiotics and growth hormones, and processed organic foods usually contain only organic ingredients.[14] You can recognize it (most of the time) by its round USDA Organic sticker and a code number that begins with the number 9.

Why doesn't everybody spare themselves exposure to harmful chemicals and other pollutants by eating organic foods only? Mainly because organic foods are almost always more expensive and may be hard to find in some stores.

🍴 "I'M THE SCARECROW"

Mohammed Hussain, age sixteen, serves an important function in his grandmother's organic garden.

My family lives in a house with a plot of land behind it. When we moved there, my grandmother, who lives with us, decided to grow some edible plants. Since then, every spring, my grandmother decides what will be produced and, along with my younger sisters, she makes some holes in the dirt and plants seeds.

I'll help out occasionally—getting down and dirty working with the soil has always been fun. But my main task is that I am really the scarecrow. Squirrels have been a major problem, because they come into our garden and scoop out the planted seeds. As the scarecrow, my job is to alert my grandmother. If one comes by, my grandmother, younger sisters, and I will scare them away. I once ran outside brandishing a broom—although a comical scene, it worked.

Watching the garden is worth it. My grandmother has planted black, red, and green peppers; lima beans; red spinach; and pumpkins. I've eaten many of our garden-grown plants. I have never actually noticed the difference in taste between our homegrown edibles and those bought from a supermarket. That may be because my taste buds aren't all that great.

But I do know the satisfaction that comes with growing our own food. When I get older, I plan on one day owning a house with a large backyard. There I plan to continue growing my own edibles. But on my agenda is planting one thing my grandmother doesn't: watermelons. A garden cannot be called a garden without watermelons.

Mohammed Hussein says, "I know the satisfaction that comes with growing your own food."

HOW TO RECOGNIZE ORGANIC LABELS[15]

The most reliable way to be sure an item is certified organic is to check the PLU (Product Look-Up) code number, printed on its sticker. If it is organic, the PLU code number should begin with the number 9. Codes of nonorganic food begin with the number 4.

As mentioned earlier, starting back in the 1950s food became more plentiful and cheaper partly because of the widespread use of chemical pesticides and fertilizers. It's taken a few decades for scientists, and the rest of us, to realize the downside to plentiful, cheap food. Chemicals have helped us produce more but at the expense of endangering ourselves and the environment.

To detect whether produce is certified organic, make sure the last number of the sticker code is 9.

Two Sides of the Story

Let's assume you'd prefer to eat foods produced in the healthiest manner. Most people would, just as most people are in favor of regulations that protect health. So why don't we have laws requiring all farming to be organic? For one thing, not everyone agrees about the superiority of organic food. Some people are outright opponents. Even the USDA, the agency in charge of these matters, has this point of view: "USDA makes no claims that organically produced food is safer or more nutritious than conventionally produced food. Organic food differs from conventionally grown food in the way it is grown, handled, and processed."[16]

Nutritionist Marion Nestle doesn't like the USDA's position on this subject. According to her, politicians are too ready to favor conventional (nonorganic) growers.[17] Why would that be? First, some well-intended politicians are willing to sacrifice naturalness in foods for the chance to feed more people at lower cost. Second, other politicians, looking out for the economic interests of their supporters (manufacturers of pesticides and fertilizers), believe their supporters will lose money if organic food replaces fertilized food.

In spite of roadblocks, more and more people are becoming aware of potential harm caused by agricultural chemicals. Since the early 1990s the rate of organic food production has only grown 20 percent a year. That sounds pretty good, but progress is actually slow. As of April 2008 organic food accounted for only 1–2 percent of food sales in the whole world.[18] Still, organic foods have become a big business. They're now available in many regular supermarkets, and "nearly two-thirds of American shoppers bought at least one organic food product in 2005."[19]

Cost of Organic Food

Economic hard times, of course, can affect the purchase of organic foods. If your family—of eight, let's say, with guests—had made a completely organic Thanksgiving dinner in 2008, you would have spent $295.36, or *75 percent more* than for a comparable nonorganic dinner.[20] On a daily basis there are young mothers like Joni Heard, in Florida, who say they can't justify spending more for organic foods as long as there's uncertainty about a husband's job. Some organic enthusiasts claim they'll cut back on vacations, cars, and restaurants in order to continue to buy organic foods.[21]

How Great Is Cost?

Some critics claim that growing food organically results in less output, but a 1981 study showed that organic farmers reported only small declines in yields, and those were offset by lower fuel costs. More recent studies show that organic farms are nearly as productive as nonorganic, are healthier for the soil, and use energy more efficiently.[22] In other words, the price to consumers for organic foods shouldn't be very different from nonorganic. Unfortunately, at this point, prices to consumers for organic foods are substantially higher than for nonorganic.

Now let's talk about you and your family personally. Is it worth to spend a little more for organic foods? You may decide they taste better. Even though organic produce may not look as perfect as the sprayed apple or tomato, taste is often improved.

In terms of nutrition, "no conclusive evidence shows that organic food is more nutritious than is conventionally grown food,"[23] according to Mayo Clinic researchers, and a two-year study in Denmark found no difference between nutrients in organic versus nonorganic produce. But as is usually the case, researchers don't all agree. A 2007 study published in the *Journal of Agriculture and Food Chemistry* suggests that organic foods—especially tomatoes—contain almost twice as many nutrients as nonorganic.[24]

Safety in Organics

You'd expect organic foods to be safer than nonorganic. The trouble is, even though organics are healthier because they aren't tainted with pesticides, *organic* doesn't necessarily rule out contamination from rodent droppings, mold, and salmonella. Contaminated peanut butter from Texas and Georgia that caused a recent panic happened to have federal organic certification.

Who decides if a product is certified organic? Inspectors, working for various organizations, companies, and state governments, who have been deputized by the federal government. The problem is that some of these certifiers are paid by the farmers and manufacturers who are being inspected, which means the certifiers have something to lose if they deny certification. Meanwhile the Organic Trade Association is set on keeping up its reputation by promoting organics on its website and working for higher standards.[25]

Twenty Pounds of Pesticides

So, if organic foods aren't proven to be more nutritious and they don't look as good, why spend the extra money? Because organically grown foods have lower levels of pesticides. And although some governmental officials claim pesticides are safe, nutritionist Marion Nestle says, "Pesticides are demonstrably harmful to farm workers and wildlife, and they accumulate in soils for ages. If they kill pests, can they be good for you? If they were really that benign, there would be no reason for the government to bother to regulate them, but it does."[26]

Can we count on the federal government to regulate pesticides? The answer isn't clear. The FDA estimates that twenty pounds of pesticides per person per year are used in the United States At least fifty of these pesticides are classified as cancer-causing.[27] Why are fifty cancer-causing chemicals tolerated? As usual, because certain business interests have been able to influence those who make the laws. In other words, the Environmental Protection Agency may as well be saying, "We realize that pesticides are a threat to humans, but the economic benefit outweighs the potential hazard."

If you and your family are worried about the long-term effects of agricultural chemicals, you may want to stick with organic products, especially in the case of yourself and younger kids. A small amount of pesticide residue probably won't kill

Grandma, but what about pesticide buildup over your lifetime or the lifetime of a baby?

Greene's Challenge

While you're considering whether to limit yourself to organic foods, a California pediatrician and author, Dr. Alan Greene, decided to conduct an experiment on himself. For three years he ate nothing, at home or out, that wasn't organic. Eating at home wasn't so hard, but locating restaurants that would accommodate him was so tough that on the road he had to carry packages of organic backpacking food. Aside from scientific curiosity, Greene was originally motivated by the discovery that dairy cows got sick less often when they were switched to organic feed.

What did Dr. Greene decide about eating organic only, after doing it for three years? He came to these conclusions: (1) He has more energy. (2) He wakes up earlier. (3) He catches fewer illnesses from his kiddie patients. And (4) he produces urine of a brighter yellow color—a sign that he's taking in more vitamins and nutrients.[28]

Can You Trust Those Organic Labels?

Let's say Dr. Greene inspires you and you decide to go organic. Can you trust that certified organic label, which supposedly means produce has been grown according to principles established by the Organic Foods Production Act of 1990 and by USDA Organic Standards of 2002? These standards, according to Marion Nestle, "take up hundreds of pages in the *Federal Register* and do not make for light reading." Loose interpretation of these guidelines, according to Nestle, can result in occasional confusion, and yet she believes that cheating is rare and labels are trustworthy.[29]

Organic Meats

When it comes to organic meat, by the way, USDA standards for organic are rigorous and complicated. You may have trouble in many markets finding certified organic meat. Meat labeled "all natural" may be good, but it isn't organic. For meat to be organic the animal must have been fed organically grown grain, allowed freedom of movement outdoors, and raised without using antibiotics, hormones, or other animal drugs. Prices of organic meats are obviously high.

More Complications

If you want to buy organic and see no label, you shouldn't necessarily reject produce. Because the certification process is so bureaucratic, expensive, and complicated, some organic farmers sell their products without bothering with certification. In other words, there is such a thing as *unlabeled* organic. According to Cindy Burke in *To Buy or Not to Buy Organics*, if you want the healthiest, safest food, get to know the people who bring it to you and go with advice of those you trust.[30]

NOTES

1. U.S. Food and Drug Administration, "Teen Science Classes Serve Up Lessons in Food Safety," FDA Consumer, www.fda.gov/FDAC/features/2002/102_teen.html (accessed January 7, 2008).

2. "Food Poisoning," Medline Plus, www.nlm.nih.gov/medlineplus/ency/article/001652.htm (accessed December 16, 2008).

3. "Food Poisoning: Salmonella," Answers.com, www.answers.com/topic/food-poisoning-salmonella (accessed December 17, 2008).

4. Robert Tauxe, "Health Alert," *Bottom Line Health Magazine*, April 15, 2007, 11–12.

5. "The Biggest Beef Recall Ever," Editorial, *New York Times*, February 21, 2008, A22.

6. Tauxe, "Health Alert," 12.

7. Marian Burros, "Who's Watching What We Eat?" *New York Times*, May 16, 2007, F1.

8. "Food and Drug Administration (United States)," Wikipedia, en.wikipedia.org/wiki/Food_and_Drug_Administration (accessed December 11, 2008).

9. "The Biggest Beef Recall Ever," A22.

10. "Grading Progress on Food Safety," Editorial, *New York Times*, December 6, 2008, www.nytimes.com/2008/12/06/opinion/06sat2.html (accessed December 11, 2008).

11. Leonard Chung, "Unsafe Beef," *The Record* (Bergen County, NJ), May 21, 2008.

12. Gardiner Harris, "President Plans Team to Overhaul Food Safety," *New York Times*, March 15, 2009.

13. "Irradiation: Expensive, Ineffective, and Impractical," www.foodandwaterwatch.org/food/foodirradiation/irradiation-facts (accessed December 16, 2008).

14. "Organic Food," Wikipedia, 1, en.wikipedia.org/wiki/Organic_food (accessed November 14, 2008).

15. Cindy Burke, *To Buy or Not to Buy Organics* (New York: Marlowe, 2007), 38.

16. Marion Nestle, *What to Eat* (New York: North Point Press, 2006), 42.

17. Nestle, *What to Eat*, 43.

18. "Organic Food," 1.

19. Burke, *To Buy or Not to Buy Organic*, 1.

20. Tara Parker-Pope, "Well," *New York Times*, December 2, 2008, D5.

21. "Budgets Squeezed, Some Families Bypass Organics," *New York Times*, October 31, 2008, 2, www.nytimes.com/2008/11/01/business/01organic.html?pagewanted=2&_r=1 (accessed November 22, 2008).

22. Nestle, *What to Eat*, 44–45.

23. Mayo Clinic staff, "Organic Foods: Are They Safer? More Nutritious?" MayoClinic.com, www.mayoclinic.com/health/organic-food/NU00255 (accessed November 22, 2008).

24. Parker-Pope, "Well," D5.

25. Kim Severson and Andrew Martin, "It's Organic, but Does That Mean It's Safer?" *New York Times*, March 4, 2009, D1, D5.

26. Nestle, *What to Eat*, 45.

27. Burke, *To Buy or Not to Buy Organic*, 12–13.

28. Parker-Pope, "Well," D5.

29. Nestle, *What to Eat*, 42.

30. Burke, *To Buy or Not to Buy Organic*, xvi.

8 **Want to Cook?**

"**I** started cooking as a teenager," says Robb Walsh, author of *Are you Really Going to Eat That?* As the oldest of six sons, he was expected to make dinner when his parents went away for the weekend, and he started enjoying it. With only one cookbook in the house, he began trying his own recipes.[1] At that point, growing up in Connecticut, Walsh didn't know he'd eventually be referred to as "the Indiana Jones of food writers" as a result of his explorations in eating everything from armadillo to zebra.

For Walsh, cooking that began in because he had to ended in a great interest and a lifetime career. Meanwhile writer Peg Bracken turned a supposed dislike of cooking into a career. Her 1960 *The I Hate to Cook Book*—humorous, illustrated, and emphasizing speed, economy, and convenience—sold more than 3 million copies by the time she died at age eighty-nine in 2007.

ARE COOKS BORN OR MADE?

Do you see yourself as someone who likes to cook, right now or someday? Anelys Fernandez, age seventeen, says "I've been a fan of the kitchen since I was little, helping my mom cut vegetables and pretending I was a renowned chef with my own mini-series. I spend much of my time watching the Food Network or typing out new recipes."

Encouragement at an early age may get kids off to a promising start. Robb Walsh, for instance, grew up watching his grandmother turn a twenty-five-pound sack of flour into flatbread and strudel. And at age five, Renee Cavallo, originator of a Boston-area cooking school called Create-a-Cook, followed her father to his restaurant.[2]

"My grandmother started teaching me how to cook when I was 5 or 6," says blogger "courty21." Fellow blogger "Takenfor" says, "My dad's a chef and my mom's a waitress, so I've grown up in restaurants. . . . I started to try new things when I was about 17, because I got sick of the food my mom was making. . . . Now I cook dinner for my family about once a month and dinner for my boyfriend once a week."[3]

"I love to bake and cook just about everything. I find a lot of my recipes on food blogs or Tastespotting.com, a website that shows pictures of GORGEOUS food with links to recipes."
—Sarah, age sixteen

Still, thousands of kids blessed with great role models can't boil an egg and don't want to. If you're among them, don't feel bad. Lots of people gradually develop a need for, or interest in, cooking. Just because you're not in the kitchen at this point doesn't mean you won't love being there someday.

WHO'S COOKING?

Generations of moms and grandmas have passed along cooking tips. Notice the emphasis on females—a tradition that dates back to cavemen bringing meat home and cavewomen tending the fire. Only since the 1960s, with the arrival of modern feminism, have large numbers of women protested. Why should mom always have to make dinner, especially if she has a full-time job? And there's the ironic point often noted by those same protesting women—how come, until recently, world-class chefs were always men?

The trend seems to be reversing. A growing number of women are gaining fame as chefs, and many men are routinely found in the kitchen. Yahoo blogger "Cap'n Jack" says, "I'll be 17 in a month and I always do the cooking at home. Chicken parm, shrimp scampi. Whatever my parents ask for all I need is a recipe and I can do it."[4]

FAMILY GATEKEEPER

Who's the primary cook in your family—a parent, a grandparent, a nanny, yourself? This "nutritional gatekeeper," the one who buys and prepares most of the food, influences more than 70 percent of what family members eat. At one point health researchers thought husbands and children influenced family diet most, but recent studies indicate it's the one who shops and cooks. And that person's personality, cooking methods, and favorite ingredients determine to a great extent how healthily the family eats. Cornell University researchers who questioned 770 families came up with five basic types:

1. **Giving cooks (specialize in comfort food)**
2. **Methodical cooks (stick to cookbooks)**
3. **Competitive cooks (try to impress)**
4. **Healthy cooks (emphasize health over taste)**
5. **Innovative cooks (like to experiment)**

Knowing what type you are can help you recognize your biases.[5]

In many private cooking classes, which have become popular teenage alternatives to a movie or night at the mall, males are almost as likely to enroll as females. "Instead of throwing a dance party, we just wanted to hang out and cook," says San Francisco high school football player Rodney Hampton-Wise.[6]

COOKING AS ENTERTAINMENT

The Culinary Institute of America at Astor Center in New York City recently offered a sold-out class for teens that focused on comfort foods. "We now have more teen classes than ever before on our calendar," says Culinary Institute educator Kelly Ann Hargrove. "The demand is there because food today is entertainment. Teens watch the Food Network and they aspire to do what they see. And there's the celebrity angle driving the trend, too. Kids think of celebrity chefs the way they used to think of sports figures."[7]

REQUIRED COOKING CLASSES IN SCHOOL

Talk to your parents or grandparents and you'll probably hear stories about required courses they took in middle and high school, such as shop (industrial arts), sewing, and cooking. Courses like these, popular after World War II, were useful but came to be seen in the late 1960s as sexist. At first, many school systems reacted to that criticism by requiring males as well as females to take home economics courses. "By the late 1970s one-third of male high school graduates had some home-ec training," in contrast to only 3.5 percent in 1962.[8]

Since then, however, home economics has been dropped or cut back in many schools. Lack of money and changing attitudes have resulted in far fewer kids taking cooking classes in high school—and not only fewer boys but fewer girls, too.[9]

Jennifer Bozek, teacher in Teaneck, New Jersey, instructs her level-2 cooking class.

Rahmiel Brown prepares wontons in his high school cooking class.

Journalist Jennifer Grossman would love to see the return of home economics courses in public schools. "Before you choke on your 300-calorie, trans-fat-laden Krispy Kreme," she says, "consider: teaching basic nutrition and food preparation is a far less radical remedy than gastric bypass surgery."[10] She'd like to see home economics courses required and revised for the twenty-first century that would include teaching kids about the dangers of food additives and the benefits of antioxidants.

EXCEPTIONAL HIGH SCHOOL PROGRAMS

Even if required cooking classes are an endangered species in the United States, serious chef training is flourishing in some schools. Teaneck High School in New Jersey offers four levels of elective classes. After students learn basics, they take on specialties, such as pastry-making, use of herbs, and international cooking. The fourth-year class runs a food operation in collaboration with the school's business department. Some students use the program as a springboard to food service careers.

New York City, in 2004, opened its Food and Finance High School, where about 600 students, some economically deprived, focus on both culinary skills and the usual academics. Kids in English class read *Fast Food Nation*, by Eric Schlosser. They learn math partially through measuring ingredients. According to Richard Grausman, president of the Careers through Culinary Arts Program, "other schools around the country are considering similar curriculums."[11]

COOKING BECAUSE YOU LIKE TO

Do you know kids who just plain love to cook? Rodney Hampton-Wise would rather cook with friends once a month than go to a nightclub or the mall. By the time you read this, Nyasia Hoskins, seventeen, a vegetarian living with her grandparents in the Bronx, New York, will have made, several times, her favorite Filipino noodle dish called pansit, and nineteen-year-old Sherri Khatami, in Dallas, Texas, will have served her own Iranian specialties to 100 guests at a graduation party.[12]

And these teenage cooks aren't necessarily rare exceptions. Gail Brousal, head of St. Ann's High School in Brooklyn, New York, says that the number of students at St. Ann's who are seriously interested in cooking is on the rise. She attributes this interest to more greenmarkets, kids' greater familiarity with restaurants, and the wave of food television shows and magazines to which they're exposed.[13]

COOKING CLASSES THAT CHARGE TUITION

Let's say you don't know a grape leaf from a piece of arugula. You have no in-house role model and no cooking courses at school—but you're anxious to learn. Some schools and youth groups sponsor cooking clubs, but if none are available, and you or your parents are willing to pay, private classes aimed at teenagers are gaining in popularity. Some, like the Young Chefs program at the Culinary Institute of America in Hyde Park, New York, are geared to kids who hope to be chefs. But many, according to Liv Grey, founder of an operation called Medium Rare in suburban New York City, are just looking for basic knowledge and fun. "I started with simple things like cookies and muffins, and it's just taken off from there," Grey says. "Now, especially with teens, we're talking sushi-making parties, Chinese, Mexican, you name it."[14]

Some classes stress the relationship between the growing of food and the preparation of it. "I think it's important that we understand the food chain," Grey says. "Food doesn't just come from a grocery store. I want [kids] to know there's grit and dirt involved." In that spirit, the Stone Barns Center for Food and Agriculture in Pocantico Hills, New York, offers farm-to-table classes for families on weekends all year long.[15]

Some cooking courses and camps are expensive. But regardless of where you live, the odds are you'll find an affordable situation. Classes are often offered in evening adult-school programs or in YWCAs, such as one in western Massachusetts. In Portland, Oregon, you'll find classes specializing in the cooking of low-budget meals. Go on the Internet to discover the possibilities in your area.

IF YOU WANT A COOKING CAREER

School guidance counselors may be helpful. One way to get the big picture is to examine a book such as *Food Jobs: 150 Great Jobs for Culinary Students, Career Changers and Food Lovers*, by Irena Chalmers.[16] Here you'll find job descriptions, anecdotes from experienced professionals, and information about culinary programs.

🍴 GET A CULINARY EDUCATION!

Christina Cassel, age nineteen, is an intern at Loaves and Fishes, in Sagaponack, New York. She's currently studying culinary arts at Johnson and Wales University in Providence, Rhode Island.

My responsibilities at Loaves and Fishes involve helping customers with food choices. I gather meats, vegetables, breads, pastries, and cheeses and ring up the orders. The most enjoyable part of the job for me is working with pastries and breads, since I'm studying baking and pastry in college. The most challenging thing is working with cheeses. There are so many things to learn about them and so much to learn about pairing them with other foods and beverages.

I got interested in food in the first place because my mother did a lot of baking. She taught me so much, and working also helps. Loaves and Fishes is a great place to learn. And now, my education has really developed me even more.

I want to do two years of baking and two years of culinary with a minor in business. Then I'd like to get my master's in teaching so I can be a culinary arts teacher in high school.

Christina Cassel, a culinary arts student, slices cake at Loaves and Fishes in Sagaponack, New York.

And obviously, go to the Internet. For those interested in careers in food service, the American Culinary Federation Foundation Accrediting Commission (online) currently lists 169 formal training programs in the United States. These programs, offered in many cities, aren't limited to chef-training only. People interested in all kinds of food-service jobs attend in order to learn about menu planning, nutrition, proper food storage, purchasing, banquet service, and more.

Recent statistics show that going for a career in food service is practical because (1) the food industry in the United States provides jobs for more than 12.2 million employees, and (2) by 2014 the restaurant industry will need an additional 1.5 million workers to meet demands.[17]

THAT COMPETITIVE EDGE

Look for "cooking competitions for teens" on an Internet search engine and you'll find more than 130,000 entries. How come there are so many contests? Food educators and marketers sense that teenagers, in general, like competition. TV producers have also taken advantage of this interest by creating programs like the Bravo Channel's *Junior Top Chef*. A lot of kids enter contests as an entrée to a career. Others just want a chance to appear on TV.

Speaking of prizes, probably the most respected cooking prize in the world is the Bocuse d'Or trophy, given in an annual competition in Lyon, France. As of 2009, no American has taken higher than sixth place.

SCHOLARSHIPS

If a young cook wants a chance at a solid culinary education, the San Diego–based Art Institute's Best Teen Chef Competition, now in its tenth year, is offering more than $250,000 in scholarships. "In addition to a full-tuition scholarship and the title of Best Teen Chef, the national first place winner, in partnership with Food Network, will be an 'Intern for a Day' at Food Network Kitchens in New York

137

City." The International Culinary Schools at the Art Institutes, sponsors of this competition, is North America's biggest system of cooking programs—found in thirty locations. To learn how to enter the Best Teen Chef Competition, visit www.artinstitutes.edu/pr.aspx?ID=btc092.[18]

Many other special programs exist, such as a full-tuition scholarship offered by the Classic Cooking Academy in Scottsdale, Arizona, to "a promising Native American student." Pascal Dionot, chef and executive director of the program, hopes to encourage culinary education in the Native American community because the need for native foods, managed by native peoples, is vast.[19]

WHAT'S THE BEST TRAINING FOR CHEFS?

Although anybody can set up a cooking class, some schools and programs have much higher standards than others. According to the website cookingschools.com, there is no objective ranking of cooking schools. "While it's true that there are a few very well-known and respected culinary schools that are on the tip of nearly every professional chef's tongue, the answer to the question 'what's best for me' will be different for every individual."[20]

Some of those best known culinary schools include the Culinary Institute of America, in Hyde Park, New York; the French Culinary Institute and the Italian Culinary Academy, in New York City; Le Cordon Bleu, with schools in Pasadena, California, and twelve other North American locations; the International Culinary Schools at the Art Institutes, found in thirty cities; and Johnson and Wales University in Providence, Rhode Island.

P.S. Be cautious about rave reviews of cooking schools on the Internet, because many of those "reviews" are posted by the schools themselves. If you're seriously interested in a program, in addition to reading about it, visit the school and talk to present or former students.

GOING ABROAD

Since the United States is a latecomer to the banquet in terms of appreciating the finest in food, serious American students often attend schools outside this country. France and Italy have long been destinations for chefs-in-training. These days, international interest is expanding as never before, as shown, for example, by an exchange between teenage catering students from Huddersfield, England, and Hangzhou, China. English students trained in Chinese cooking and Chinese students studied in England.[21]

LIE ON THE COUCH AND LEARN

If you can't arrange to go to Pasadena or China, there's a lot to learn about cooking from watching television. A Yahoo! directory lists more than fifty TV cooking shows, including *How to Boil Water*, *Dutch Oven & Camp Cooking*, and *Naked Chef*. According to TV critic Alessandra Stanley, "There are more cooking show variations than there are varieties of vegetable."[22]

In addition to the Food Network (begun in 1993), cooking shows appear on PBS (Public Broadcasting System), the Style Network, Bravo, MSNBC, and the Discovery Channel. Stanley says people find cooking shows gratifying because, even as celebrity chefs duke it out against unknown challengers, a sideline commentator is always there, whispering useful hints to the ordinary viewer. If you want to eat well, she says, you're best off cooking your own food, so that watching cooking shows isn't just a soothing pastime but a path to good eating.[23]

How Relevant Are These Shows?

Prime-time television being what it is, high drama, competition, and gorgeous settings are required, so that step-by-step cooking lessons, once typical on TV, are now usually scheduled in less popular viewing hours. Shows like *Top Chef* on Bravo play up suspense. Will there be a first woman Top Chef, or a first openly gay? Food writer Frank Bruni says, about another popular show, "Cooking as contest, cooking as derring-do: that pretty much sums up *Iron Chef America*, on which Mr. [Bobby] Flay and Mr. [Mario] Batali have been mainstays. It's colorful. It's kinetic. But it has limited relevance to the home cook." And it has little connection to what cooking is like in actual restaurants.[24]

CELEBRITY CHEFS

If you get to be extremely well-known for your style of cooking, you may someday be referred to as a celebrity chef. Such chefs have created original recipes that taste great and look beautiful. Until recently only a few chefs have been known by name. The term *celebrity chef* came into everyday use in the 1990s with the great popularity of cooking shows on television, widespread publication of books by chefs, and media attention given to their restaurants. According to Wikipedia, the term is sometimes used in a derogatory way, meaning someone who has sold out to the media.[25]

NAME THAT CHEF![26]

Antoine Careme—Considered to be first celebrity chef; died in 1833

James Beard—Considered the father of American-style cooking; a foundation named for him gives cooking scholarships and awards; died in 1985

Julia Child—Inspired many Americans to cook by way of her books and enthusiastic TV demonstrations; died in 2004

Wolfgang Puck—Austrian born; gained fame with restaurant Spago in Los Angeles and now owns many other fine-dining brands

Gordon Ramsay—English; winner of fourteen Michelin stars, the highest rating for chefs

Emeril Lagasse—Came to fame on the Food Network with shows *Emeril Live* and *Essence of Emeril*

Mario Batali—Culinary school dropout, now master of Italian cuisine; owns many restaurants in New York, Los Angeles, and Las Vegas

Bobby Flay—Host on Food Network; known for Southwestern cooking

Rachael Ray—Averages over 2 million viewers a day on her four Food Network programs; known for economy and practicality

Alice Waters—Creator of restaurant Chez Panisse in Berkeley, California; promotes use of local, fresh ingredients and cooking education

But celebrity chef Emeril Lagasse (seen on the Food Network) accepts the label as a compliment. In the past "Chefs weren't really respected other than being in the kitchen. . . . You rarely saw them in the dining room interacting with people. . . . Now all of a sudden, people have started looking at chefs and saying, 'Wow! That person is really a craftsman, is really a business person, they can do publicity.'"[27]

Editor of the former *Gourmet* magazine Ruth Reichl explains the term *celebrity chef* in this way: "Many diners are seeking a personal connection as much as a good meal. The more people can identify with these chefs, the more they want to go to their places, buy their books, have some kind of contact with them."[28]

And Linda Carucci, curator of the American Center for Food, Wine and the Arts in Napa, California, thinks that the rise of celebrity chefs has drawn more men to her cooking classes. "They talk about their favorite chefs the way other guys might talk about football stars," she says.[29]

COOKBOOKS

Before cooking classes got so popular, before TV schedules were crammed with cooking shows, there were cookbooks. Back in 1896 Fannie Farmer wrote one that has sold 3.2 million copies. Best sellers of all time are cookbooks created by Betty Crocker in the 1950s (sales of 45 million) and a runner-up, *The Joy of Cooking*, with 14 million sold.[30]

Popular Cookbooks

"There are a lot of cookbooks in our hungry world," says reviewer and restaurant critic Sam Sifton, "and they keep on coming, every season, thick and glossy." In 2007, for instance, nearly 14 million books about cooking and entertaining were purchased in the United States, to the tune of $530 million dollars.[31] Amazon.com lists nearly 92,000 cookbooks. It's a relief then to look on Amazon for "cookbooks for teenagers" and find the number reduced to a mere 85.

POPULAR COOKBOOKS

Bestsellers through the Years

Betty Crocker's New Cookbook, by Betty Crocker (Macmillan, 2002)

Better Homes and Gardens Cookbook, three-ring binder 12th ed., ed. Jan Miller, and *Better Homes and Gardens Junior Cookbook*, ed. Jan Miller, published by the magazine in many editions

The James Beard Cookbook, by James Beard (Marlowe & Company, 2002; originally published in 1996)

The Joy of Cooking, 75th anniversary ed., by Irma S. Rombauer, Marion Rombauer Becker, and Ethan Becker (Scribner, 2006)

Mastering the Art of French Cooking, 40th ed., by Julia Child, Louisette Bartholle, Simone Beck, and Sidonie Coryn (Alfred A. Knopf, 2000; originally published in 1961)

Moosewood Cookbook Classics, mini ed., by Mollie Katzen (Running Press, 1996)

The Silver Palate Cookbook, 25th anniversary ed., by Julee Ross and Sheila Lukins (Workman, 2007)

More Recent Favorites

How to Cook Everything, by Mark Bittman (John Wiley & Sons, 2008)

O, the Oprah Magazine Cookbook, by the editors of *Oprah* magazine (Hyperion, 2008)

Rachael Ray 365: No Repeats, by Rachael Ray (Clarkson Potter, 2005)

Geared to Teens

Better Homes and Gardens Junior Cookbook, ed. Jan Miller (published by the magazine in many editions)

Clueless in the Kitchen, by Evelyn Raab (Firefly, 1998)

Teens Cooking: How to Cook What You Want to Eat, by Megan and Jill Carle with Judi Carle (Ten Speed Press, 2004)

Just because the whole country is devouring cookbooks, does that mean you need them? Books certainly aren't the only route to learning new skills, but even if you have a relative to teach you, a cooking class membership, and access to TV food shows, it can't hurt to own a couple of books if you want to learn to cook.

Choosing a Cookbook

Chances are, no matter how interested, you're not going to run out and buy a big collection of cookbooks. There may already be a selection of cookbooks in your house. Or, when friends and relatives learn of your interest, they may lend or give you some of theirs. Let's say, though, that you'd like to pick a few for yourself. Two obvious functions of cookbooks are getting ideas about what to make and getting instructions on how to carry out those recipes. In choosing one cookbook over another, ask yourself the following questions:

1. **Do these recipes sound good? Will my family, friends, and I enjoy eating this style of cooking?**
2. **Are the pictures and layout appealing and user friendly?**
3. **Am I going to feel comfortable reading a book with this vocabulary and tone? (When cookbooks sell well, it's almost always because the author has a distinctive and appealing voice.)**

Don't pay good money for a cookbook until you've checked it out carefully. Browse in bookstores first, or take cookbooks out of the library. Before buying the latest book of a TV celebrity chef, make sure you know and like that person's values, style, and recipes. If you're a beginner, look for at least one book that claims to be basic, a book with clear directions, useful illustrations, and complete definitions of terms.

And by the way, if you're interested in cooking dietetically, check out calorie counts of recipes in cookbooks. Research shows that "even some cookbook writers have fallen victim to the supersizing trends made popular by fast-food restaurants." Between 1936 and 2006, in the seven editions of *The Joy of Cooking*, "the calorie content had surged by an average of 928 calories, or 44 percent per recipe."[32]

COOKING ADVICE FROM THE INTERNET

The Internet is a huge source of information about specific cookbooks, but you'll face the same problem here as in the matter of cooking schools. That is, compliments about these books are often coming from the sellers themselves. Still, the Internet is a treasure trove. On Amazon.com you can look for cookbooks by category—beginners, teenage, vegetarian, French, desserts, and so on—and you can sometimes access actual pages, so that your judgment is based on knowledge.

The Internet is also useful for looking up recipes. Thousands of instructions are available at a click. On some sites (at a charge, perhaps) you can get instant answers to personal questions. "My turkey's already too brown on the top! What should I do?" On the whole, though, printing out recipes is time-consuming and the printouts are temporary. If you intend to repeat what you've made, recipes in book form work best.

IN THE KITCHEN AT LAST

So far we've barely said a word about stepping into the kitchen. If your family is encouraging you, you're lucky, because smooth sailing there isn't always a given. Teenager Rodney Hampton-Wise says, "I like being the only person in the kitchen." Liz Broadwin, a sophomore, says, "My parents make a lot of mess when they cook, but I try to do the opposite." And Sherri Khatami comments, "At Christmas, I decided I was going to cook. But what ended up happening is, my mother came in and took over. I have to be in the learning mode rather than the take-control mode for us to get along in the kitchen."[33]

Some kids, of course, like collaborating. "I have more memories of baking with my mom than I do of cooking," Caroline, age sixteen, says. "My favorite part of the experience is the final minutes when we get to try our concoction and be rewarded or else laugh at how bad it is." Lauren Grossman, host/producer of *Food, Family & Home Matters* on MSNBC, would approve of Caroline and her mom. "Real home cooking can bring a family together and inject a healing calm into even the most hectic household," she says.[34]

Basic Equipment

You're probably limited at this point to using the kitchen where you live, but maybe you'll design a great kitchen for yourself someday. Meanwhile the choice of bowls, knives, pots, pans, food processors, and other appliances and tools does matter. *Clueless in the Kitchen*, by Evelyn Raab, speaks specifically to teenagers on these matters. In his chapter

"Kitchen Basics," Mark Bittman, author of *How to Cook Everything*, gives good advice on equipment.[35]

Sanitary Cooking

By now you've certainly watched someone else cook—in person or on television. Or maybe you've read instructions in a book or on the Internet. You've brought in the ingredients, set up equipment, and are ready to go. Some of the following advice is obvious, but just in case, don't forget.

1. Before you cook, wash your hands well with soap and warm water. Wash again anytime you handle raw meat or poultry.

2. Keep your work area uncluttered and clean. Wash the countertops, sink, and drain often with a commercial cleaning agent.

3. Wash fruits and vegetables thoroughly in warm water.

4. Wash lids of canned foods before opening, clean can opener after each use, and clean the food processor as soon as you finish using it.

5. Use clean utensils and wash them between uses with different foods.

6. Avoid putting cooked—or any—food on an unwashed plate that held raw meat.

7. Keep dishcloths and sponges clean by washing them in a washing machine or heating then in a microwave.

NOTES

1. Robb Walsh, *Are You Really Going to Eat That? Reflections of a Culinary Thrill Seeker* (New York: Counterpoint, 2003), xiii.

2. Kate Barreira, "No More Takeout: The Kids Are Cooking Dinner," *Boston Globe*, March 1, 2006, www.boston.com/ae/food/articles/2006/03/01/no_more_takeout_the_kids_are_cooking_dinner (accessed November 12, 2008).

3. "How Many of You Teens Can Cook, Really Cook, Follow Recipes, Plan a Weeks Meals and Shop for Them?" Yahoo! Answers, 2, answers.yahoo.com/question/index?qid=20081006080256AAd4l mO (accessed January 19, 2009).

4. "How Many of You Teens Can Cook," 4.

5. Tara Parker-Pope, "Who's Cooking? (For Health, It Matters)," *New York Times*, March 17, 2009, D6.

6. Matt Lee and Ted Lee, "10th Grade, Four Courses and Dessert," *New York Times*, May 29, 2002, 2, www.nytimes.com/2002/05/29/dining/10th-grade-four-courses-and-dessert.html (accessed November 12, 2008).

7. Rosemary Black, "Cooking Classes a Hot New Hobby for Kids and Teens," *New York Daily News*, September 20, 2008, www.nydailynews.com/lifestyle/food/2008/09/20/2008-09-20_cooking_classes_a_hot_new_hobby_for_kids.html (accessed November 12, 2008).

8. Jennifer Grossman, "Food for Thought (and for Credit)," *New York Times*, September 2, 2003, www.nytimes.com/2003/09/02/opinion/food-for-thought-and-for-credit.html (accessed January 24, 2009).

9. Grossman, "Food for Thought (and for Credit)."

10. Grossman, "Food for Thought (and for Credit)."

11. Kim Severson, "The Teacher Ate My Homework," *New York Times*, April 11, 2007, www.nytimes.com/2007/04/11/dining/11school.html (accessed March 16, 2009).

12. Lee and Lee, "10th Grade, Four Courses and Dessert," 2–3.

13. Lee and Lee, "10th Grade, Four Courses and Dessert," 2–3.

14. Emily DeNitto, "Cooking Classes Preparing Young Chefs," *New York Times*, March 9, 2008, 1, www.nytimes.com/2008/03/09/nyregion/nyregionspecial2/09dinewe.html?_r=1&fta (accessed January 19, 2009).

15. DeNitto, "Cooking Classes Preparing Young Chefs," 2.

16. Irena Chalmers, *Food Jobs: 150 Great Jobs for Culinary Students, Career Changers and Food Lovers* (New York: Beaufort Books, 2008).

17. Chalmers, *Food Jobs*, 3.

18. "Win a Scholarship and be an Intern for a Day at Food Network," The Art Institute of California–San Diego, November 5, 2008, www.artinstitutes.edu/sandiego/NewsAndEvents/BTCPressrelease.aspx (accessed January 26, 2009).

19. "Culinary School Offering Scholarship to Native American Recipient," *News from Indian Country*, October 27, 2008, 20.

20. "Ranking Cooking Schools," CookingSchools, www.cookingschools.com/articles/ranking (accessed January 28, 2009).

21. Katie Campling, "Student Chefs Train-ing to Cook in China! Five Teenagers Get on the Right Track," *Huddersfield Daily Examiner* (Huddersfield, England), October 31, 2008, findarticles.com/p/articles/mi_6784/is_/ai_n30955892 (accessed January 24, 2009).

22. Alessandra Stanley, "Next Food Network Star," *New York Times*, June 24, 2005, 3, tv.nytimes.com/2005/06/24/art/television/24tvwk.html (accessed January 25, 2009).

23. Stanley, "Next Food Network Star," 3.

24. Frank Bruni, "TV Chefs, Far from Reality," *New York Times*, October 3, 2007, 3, www.nytimes.com/2007/10/03/dining/03note.html (accessed January 25, 2009).

25. "Celebrity Chef," Wikipedia, 1, en.wikipedia.org/wiki/Celebrity_chef (accessed January 26, 2009).

26. "Celebrity Chef" and Chaniga Vorasarun, "Ten Top-Earning Celebrity Chefs," Forbes, August 8, 2008, www.forbes.com/2008/08/08/celebrity-chef-earners-forbeslife-cx_cv_0808food.html (accessed January 26, 2009).

27. Ari Shapiro, "Americans' Insatiable Hunger for Celebrity Chefs, NPR, March 5, 2005, www.npr.org/templates/story/story.php?storyId=4522975 (accessed January 26, 2009).

28. Shapiro, "Americans' Insatiable Hunger for Celebrity Chefs."

29. Shapiro, "Americans' Insatiable Hunger for Celebrity Chefs."

30. "Best-Selling Cookbooks," Books and Cooks, thecooksbooks.tripod.com/bestsellers.html (accessed January 29, 2009).

31. Sam Sifton, "Cooking," *New York Times*, Sunday Book Review, June 1, 2008, 2, www.nytimes.com/2008/06/01/books/review/Sifton-Cooking-t.html (accessed January 28, 2009).

32. Parker-Pope, "Who's Cooking?" D6.

33. Lee and Lee, "10th Grade, Four Courses and Dessert," 4.

34. "Food/Lifestyle Expert Helps Parents Strength Family Bonds with Teenagers Using Home Cooking Strategy," PRWeb, October 4, 2006, www.prweb.com/releases/2006/10/prweb439594.htm (accessed January 19, 2009).

35. Evelyn Raab, *Clueless in the Kitchen* (New York: Firefly Books, 1998); Mark Bittman, *How to Cook Everything* (Hoboken, NJ: John Wiley & Sons, 2008), 1–20.

9

What Did You Eat in School Today?

What did *you* eat at school today? Maybe a lunch paid for, partly at least, by the federal government. Or something you took from home. A burger and fries from a local McFastfood? Nachos and a soda? Or did you skip lunch?

Through the years, kids have traditionally complained about cafeteria food. Has that just been a pose—kids sticking together against the common enemy, adults? Or are there legitimate complaints involved in badmouthing school food?

"In middle school I always brought my lunch! The cafeteria was horrendous and known for having hair in the food. The only items my friends ever ate from the cafeteria were the cookies, which were often undercooked and sometimes even had yolks in them. . . . In college, though, the dining hall has everything, from yogurt to sushi. I wouldn't change anything, because the dining hall is so accommodating and has great variety."

—Anne, age nineteen

"INSTITUTIONAL-STYLE MAYHEM?"

Food writers Ann Cooper and Lisa Holmes are outraged: "For the most part, school lunch has deteriorated to institutional-style mayhem. . . . USDA-approved portions of processed foods are haphazardly dished out by harried cafeteria workers to frenzied students hurrying to finish their food in time for ten minutes of recess. . . . A recent survey of school children in

"I think lunches at my school are pretty good. I usually buy a sandwich, but sometimes I get the hot meal."

—Caroline, age seventeen

"There are times when I just step out of line because the food is so bad."

—Annamarie, age seventeen

northern Minnesota revealed the food is so abysmal that not even old standby favorites like pizza and macaroni and cheese were given high marks."[1]

It's not that Cooper and Holmes are impossible to satisfy. They praise to the skies the lunch program at Ross School in East Hampton, New York, where fresh food is cooked by trained professional chefs and cooks, where there's a wood-fired pizza oven, hand-picked ceramic dishware, and a woodsy dining room view. According to Cooper and Holmes, "The Ross food experience showed that if you put delicious food in front of kids, even if it's vegetables and whole grains, they'll eat it because they're attracted to the flavors."[2]

The problem is trying to replicate the private-school Ross model in other schools. No matter how successful Ross School's lunch program is, and no matter how many scholarships they give, we can't ignore the fact that it's not a public school and tuition is high. Still, a program like Ross's may be an inspiration to other schools.

WE EAT AND WE LEARN

Hannah Newton and Noah Engel, both age fifteen, are students at Ross School in East Hampton, New York.

Hannah: Ross's food program is definitely a special experience, mainly because while enjoying new foods we get to learn about them. We're taught about sustainability and how beneficial vegetables and grains are to our diets. Every day there's a different meal, from special salads to roasted cauliflower.

Because we have a spiral curriculum at Ross everything is integrated with our Cultural History classes. This sometimes includes culinary arts studies as part of a major unit. And language classes make traditional dishes. For example, French make crepes and Chinese make dumplings. It's also nice to know the café staff listens to what we have to say, which builds a great eating environment.

Noah: At Ross, lunch is not only a place where we eat but a place where we learn. Being a student at Ross I have tried an array of dishes which originally I didn't even know existed. We get to eat regional organic foods that are prepared for us by our incredible team of chefs.

Students studying, for example, Mayan culture can sample Mayan dishes I the café. And if a student has a particular love or passion for culinary arts, he or she can take part in preparing meals for the other students and staff.

Hannah Newton and Noah Engel, in the café at Ross School, East Hampton, New York, like the way food studies are integrated into their school's spiral curriculum.

CREDIT—AND BLAME—FOR SCHOOL FOOD

Criticism of most school food keeps coming. Sam Kass, the Chicago chef appointed by President Barack Obama to be White House cook, talks about "the sorry state of the National School Lunch Program." A promoter of fresh foods, Kass links high consumption of sugary foods and food additives to kids'

learning difficulties.[3] If his complaints are valid, where do we place the blame? (1) On the cafeteria ladies (occasionally men) who serve you school lunch? (2) On the administration and school board? (3) On state and federal governments? Or (4) on your parents and yourself for not protesting enough?

THE ROOTS OF SCHOOL FOOD

If some part of your school lunch tastes like it's been around for more than a hundred years, maybe it has. The earliest school lunch program in the United States began in 1853. Now let's leap ahead to the Great Depression (early 1930s), when a million school kids got free hot lunches through President Roosevelt's Works Progress Administration. By the 1960s lunch programs had two purposes—feeding kids, of course, but also using surplus foods grown by farmers who were receiving government subsidies.[4]

UPDATE ON SCHOOL LUNCH

Are you one of the more than 30 million kids per year who eats a breakfast and/or lunch subsidized by the federal government? In 2007 the National School Lunch Program (NSLP) served more than 5 billion meals. At an expense of $10.9 billion, the NSLP claims to provide nutritionally balanced low-cost or free lunches to more than 94,000 schools.[5]

Changes in the federal lunch program were ordered in 1994, so that U.S. Dietary Standards are now upheld, which translates into more fresh produce, plus a reduction of fat, sodium, and sugar content. Any student in a not-for-profit school may take advantage of the NSLP bargain, but kids from families with limited incomes are entitled to reduced-price or completely free meals.[6]

ALICE WATERS ISN'T SATISFIED

Chef, writer, and wholesome-food promoter Alice Waters doesn't think those 1994-mandated changes are good enough. According

"YO, WHAT THEY GOT?"

Annamarie Turton, age seventeen, eats her school lunch in New York City.

The biggest boys jump up from their seats and make a mad dash for the lunch line, but I always try to beat them, because I know I'll be crushed if I'm caught the stampede. The less aggressive kids step outside the kitchen door to check the menu, even though the menu is hardly ever reliable. What is actually served is usually completely different from the menu. Most kids just ask another student, "Yo, what they got?"

Kids who consider themselves popular react to school lunch in a way that surprises me. One group of girls, no matter how hungry they are, will forgo lunch because they don't want to be seen eating free food. I heard one boy say to another who was rushing out of his seat, "Do you really wanna be seen as the first one on line?" The boy ignored the comment, but a girl sat back down and waited a few minutes.

I do eat school food every day, because I can't function on an empty stomach. There are times though when I step out of line because the food is so bad. For example, once they ran out of mozzarella sticks and had only cheesy fish left. The fish and cheese make our breath stink incredibly, so I went without food until school ended.

There are some good things to be said for school food. They do serve healthy items such as fruits, milk, and vegetables, but I think they need to serve more of these things instead of treating kids to sugary ice pops or salty chips that go along with the meal. I also think they should use healthier oils to cook the food, or use a smaller amount of oil. In fact, I think the whole system should be revamped. By starting afresh, the city might avoid future problems and criticism from students and outside organizations.

Annamarie Turton thinks the cooks in her school's cafeteria should use less oil and healthier oil.

to her, the school lunch program is a bad investment and should be completely redesigned. Her criticisms are that foods provided by the government are often as low grade and high in fat as fast foods, and the government's $2.57 payment for each free lunch isn't enough to cover costs. Waters would like to see an increase in government spending to $27 billion a year, almost three times as much as at present, which, she claims would pay off the long run, savings and benefits in terms of tastiness and health.[7]

WHAT'S A TYPICAL CAFETERIA?

How would you describe your school lunch experience? High school cafeterias vary greatly, depending on size of school, number of students who actually eat there, location, funding, and nutritional philosophy. Besides federally subsidized lunches (and breakfasts), many cafeterias offer ala carte options, that is, items sold separately for which kids pay full price.

Chances are, the more kids who use a cafeteria, the more options that will be offered. In some places a lot of kids bring lunch from home. If a school allows students to leave the grounds at lunchtime, many will zoom out of there—to go home, maybe, or, more likely, to eat fast food they buy from a vendor or at a restaurant.

Part of the reason it's hard to generalize about school food is that most decisions are left up to state and local governments. Two nearby cities or towns may have completely different types of management, menus, prices, and rules for students. Maybe the good news is that, to bring about change in school food, you need to march only as far as city hall, not all the way to Washington.

NO ESCAPE

Meanwhile some systems require kids to stay in school at lunchtime. In-school lunch is said to cut down on lateness and reduce car accidents. Another benefit of in-school lunch, to cafeteria operators, is a captive audience. The school can predict pretty accurately how much food is needed and how much money will come in. On the other hand, when kids are

REQUIRED COURSE—LUNCH[8]

Which would you rather do, advanced math or lunch? In certain schools in which college acceptance is a super-high priority, kids have crammed their schedules so full that they don't stop for lunch. What they often do instead is sneak snacks into the library or chomp down sandwiches in classes, if teachers let them get away with it.

No more, say some school administrators, such as principal Jim Kaishian at Briarcliff High in New York, where student are now required to take twenty minutes off. Getting good grades isn't enough, according to Stanford psychologist Madeline Levine, who is working to relieve stress among teenagers. Developing decent eating habits is just as important.

One school determined to eliminate hunger and stress is the Woodside Priory School near San Francisco, which has added a mandatory lunch and a thirty-minute snack break. Meanwhile in nearby Palo Alto, at the all-girl Castilleja School, milk, fresh fruit, and granola bars are put out for kids all day long.

free to leave at lunchtime, cafeterias face big competition. In their attempt to win kids' business, schools typically offer imitations of brand-name fast foods, prepared, maybe, in a slightly healthier way.

THEY PROBABLY WOULD IF THEY COULD

Providers of subsidized school lunches don't have it easy. It's not as if cafeteria staffs can order whatever raw materials they want. First, they have to use government surplus foods that are sent to them. Second, they have to stay within state and federal nutritional guidelines. Third, they get reimbursed by the federal government at a fixed rate that rarely increases. Fourth, they have to come up with results tasty enough to lure kids away from the competition.

Problems abound. Let's say the government actually has a surplus of fresh fruits and vegetables. Can this produce be shipped quickly enough around the country so that it arrives before it spoils? Obviously processed foods are easier and cheaper. Four watermelons cost as much as six cases of applesauce. The melons last one day, the applesauce lasts a month. Which fruit should the school cafeteria purchase?

Certain regulations put cafeterias in a double-bind. A nutrition coordinator in New York State complains, "Districts are being told they can't use canned fruit with added sugar, but they're not being given funds to buy and offer healthier alternatives."[9]

One more hitch is that sometimes, even if fresh produce is available, school kitchens aren't prepared to deal with it. Many school kitchens "were designed for processed, rather than whole, foods. Many are not set up even to cut up vegetables or fruit."[10]

SCHOOL CAFETERIAS ARE BUSINESSES

Is the food in your school prepared right there in a school kitchen? Or is it trucked in by a small caterer or big national company hired by your school district? Even though private food services are in business to make money, if they're good, they'll deliver tasty, fairly priced meals and leave educators with more time to deal with education. But if the private services aren't good—if they cut costs and charge schools a lot—students will pay a price in well-being, in addition to the dollar cost.

FREE LUNCH

As mentioned before, the federal government would like to think that no kid goes hungry. Those whose families have limited incomes are entitled to free breakfast and lunch. How come, though, in 2008, only 37 percent of kids eligible in San Francisco took advantage of the subsidized meals? In order to qualify for free meals, students have to submit an application. This means a family must take initiative and be willing to give out private information. Even though this income information is confidential, parents may be wary.

But this wariness isn't the main reason that some eligible kids don't eat lunch. Not only in San Francisco but everywhere, kids don't like being singled out as needy. As Louis Geist, high school student body president in Balboa, California, says, "Lunchtime is the best time to impress your peers," and being seen with a subsidized meal "lowers your status."[11]

Aren't there ways to make free lunch available without embarrassing anyone? Yes—not every school has separate lines for paid and free lunches. Some cafeterias have a debit-card system that allows one set of kids to prepay while eligible kids use the same card to get free food. And yet, a highly regarded breakfast and lunch program in Philadelphia, one in which needy students don't need to fill out applications, is being terminated. Even though 121,000 students have been depending on the free and reduced-price meals, the USDA (U.S. Drug Administration) claims it needs applications to better monitor the program.[12]

RISING COSTS

Are you paying more for lunch this year? Alex, age fifteen, says, "One of the main things I would ask for is to lower the ridiculous cost of lunch." In times of economic crisis, schools have an especially tough time providing low-cost meals. Even though the USDA increased its subsidies slightly in 2008, most schools have felt the need to raise the price of lunch. The USDA is trying to help by sending more free food, including healthy snacks, but school officials say they're still in trouble, especially if they want to offer kids skim milk, whole grains, and fresh fruit.[13]

WHAT DO KIDS WANT?

Complications pop up everywhere when it comes to school food. Nutritionists want one thing. Some kids want the opposite. Most disturbing to nutritionists are kids whose lunch consists of chips and soda. Or, worse than that, kids who skip lunch.

And yet, schools can only do so much about kids' eating. By one calculation, the NSLP provides only a little more than 10 percent of all meals a student will eat in a year.[14] In other words, maybe lunch isn't so important as long as you eat well at other meals. On the other hand, why not eat well at every meal?

🍴 HOOKED

Chantal Hylton, age seventeen, once loved home-cooked meals.

When I was a child I loved eating home-cooked meals—until my grandmother introduced me to a thing called the McDonald's Kids Meal. Every time she visited she came bearing gifts and a bag of McDonald's. At first I was more interested in the toy than anything else, but then McDonald's became the only food I'd consume. The once-a-week indulgence became an everyday routine.

My family would bribe me with McDonald's. "If you want to go to McDonald's, you better do what I say!" I learned to regard McDonald's as a treat, almost like dessert, except it was dinner.

As I grew older my love for fast food went beyond McDonald's, but the feeling of reward never went away. And now, even with my knowledge of how unhealthy fast food is, I find myself teaching my two-year-old sister bad eating habits. Whenever I go to visit her I have a McDonald's bag in my hand, and when she starts to cry, I often find myself asking her, "Do you want to go to McDonald's?"

Like me, she feels that McDonald's is something special. While she enjoys Burger King and other fast-food places, she can walk right past them. We have created a monster. She hasn't learned to read yet, but she can spot the McDonald's logo anywhere.

While I can, and do, limit the amount that my sister eats at McDonald's, I wonder if it's too later to change our eating habits. McDonald's is a way of life for us. It is where I bring my sister after a long day at the park, or when I don't feel like cooking. Maybe the next generation of our family will have a better chance of escaping McDonald's, but we are hooked.

FAST FOODS LIVE ON

Let's face it. Many kids prefer the fattening stuff they're used to. Mike, age eighteen, says his school has "tried to implement healthier food choices," but his sister Jessica, age sixteen, admits, "Me and my brother enjoy junk food and don't eat very well-rounded dinners." According to *Time*, "Some school cafeterias look little different from food courts at the local mall. Many serve hamburgers and pizzas rife with full-fat meats and cheeses or simply turn the prep work over to franchises like Burger King and Papa John's."[15]

Chantal says, "I wonder if it's too late to change our eating habits."

Over the decades battles have raged between promoters of healthy food and sellers of "competitive food" in schools. For "competitive," read junk food and sodas. Sometimes states have restricted junk foods by law but haven't enforced the regulations. Many people dissatisfied with obesity rates think the federal government should get more involved. Others believe the federal government has enough problems as it is.

If your school, like some, has closed its doors to fast-food sellers, you may feel proud—or else annoyed. When Chicago Public Schools got rid of soft drinks and fatty snacks, response of student Shone Talbert was, "What they have to offer now, none of us want. It's OK to be healthy every now and then, but it shouldn't be forced on us."[16]

WILL JUNK FOOD WIN OUT?

A lot of doctors, educators, and parents are depressed about the fact that they knock themselves out trying to teach kids about nutrition and trying to get government agencies to mandate healthier school food. But in spite of the fact that the federal government spent more than $1 billion on nutrition education in 2007, these programs don't seem to be working, according to pediatrics professor Dr. Tom Baranowski. In a certain pilot program, kids who were offered free fruits and vegetables became *less* willing to eat them at the end of the trial. And in Pennsylvania, when researchers offered prizes to kids who ate fruit and vegetables, the kids went back to eating junk as soon as the prizes ran out.[17]

VENDING MACHINES AND BAKE SALES

Are soda and chips just a few steps away from your classroom? In the 1970s vending machines appeared in many public schools. Laws in 1980 limited some of the junkiest snacks (gum, sodas, certain candy), but when the National Soft Drink Association reared its head, those laws got overturned. In some cases, by the way, students weren't the only ones with a taste for soda. School administrators and boards, looking for additional money for their schools, often welcomed the sale of brand-name beverages for a cut of the profits.[18]

HOPE FOR HEALTHY FOOD?

If you're a lover of junk food, don't celebrate yet. Some promoters of good nutrition are succeeding. Baking often replaces frying these days, and organic foods have been introduced. The U.S. Department of Defense, which once supplied food only to the military, expanded its service in the 1990s and now provides fresh produce to schools in most states.[19] Besides that, in 2005, forty-two states enacted or proposed measures to limit deep-fat frying and to add healthier beverages.[20] As of 2007, New Jersey, with its 600 school districts, led the pack in legislating against high-fat foods, soda, and candy.[21] California has always been nutrition sensitive, and Kentucky also has strict regulations in place.[22]

WAR ON VENDING MACHINES

In Chicago Public Schools, "soft drinks were booted out, and water, sports drinks and juice were offered instead. Granola bars and baked chips replaced candy bars and fried chips."[23] In New Jersey 60 percent of beverages served in schools must be pure juice, milk, or water, so that drinks with higher sugar content are limited to 40 percent. And believe it or not, a few years ago the American Beverage Association recommended the elimination of soft drinks in elementary schools, restriction in middle schools, and limitation to 50 percent of choices in high school vending machines.[24] Offering to monitor themselves, they figured, might head off criticism and laws unfavorable to them.

LUNCH INSURANCE—PEANUT BUTTER[25]

What's so great about peanut butter?
It's economical, nutritious, convenient, and tasty—and healthiest when the oil is separated and not mixed in (hydrogenated).

How much do Americans eat?
About 800 million pounds a year, enough to smoothly coat the Grand Canyon.

Who invented it?
Some say Dr. John Harvey Kellogg prepared peanut meal in 1895. Others say an unnamed St. Louis doctor in the late 1800s crushed peanuts so that his patients with bad teeth could get protein.

When did peanut butter get popular?
After it was sold in 1904 at a world's fair in St. Louis. Then, at Tuskegee University, George Washington Carver developed 300 ways of using peanuts and published 125 peanut recipes in 1925.

What are potential problems with peanut butter?
In addition to causing allergic reactions, peanuts have occasionally been contaminated with salmonella. An outbreak in 2007 sickened more than 600 people, and in 2008, 500 people became sick and 8 died from eating peanut products.

BAKE SALES BITE THE DUST

One of the last stands for extreme fat and sugar is the cookie and cake stand. In California, in fact, fund-raising bake sales are becoming obsolete. Kids there are forced to raise money for clubs by conducting carwashes or selling balloon-o-grams—or else taking their brownies across the street to be sold off school grounds.[26]

EDIBLE SCHOOLYARD

Certain people and programs around the country have made outstanding contributions to school nutrition. Perhaps the best known is Alice Waters's Edible Schoolyard in Berkeley, California. Waters wants to improve kids' health and, at the same time, help them take personal responsibility for gardening and cooking. Her logic is that if you've had a hand in growing and preparing fresh food, you'll be curious enough to try it and perhaps make it a habit.

That's why students at Martin Luther King Middle School in Berkeley, some of whom had never before seen growing corn, now routinely pick the crop planted by the previous year's classes. After ten weeks of working in the garden they move into the kitchen, where they learn how to prepare foods from all harvesting seasons. Kids from diverse backgrounds give the program high marks, not only for offering tasty eating and teaching them skills, but also for fostering a sense of community among them and with their teachers.[27]

INFLUENCE OF POLITICAL LEADERS

Good and bad nutrition are running neck-and-neck in schools. By the time you read this, some cafeterias may have already made changes for the good. Optimists are encouraged by the support of the Obama administration, since the president is known to be a strong advocate of healthy eating, and the first lady has been seen contributing time to the White House vegetable garden.

EDIBLE SCHOOLYARDS TAKE ROOT

In New York City: CookShop aims at elementary-school-age children, in hopes of catching them early. CookShop has also created the SchoolFood Plus Initiative for teenagers, where "At least once a week. . . 860,000 children . . . are being served a healthy, delicious plant-based lunch item that's been prepared with food grown in the region."[28]

Another outgrowth of the initiative is an after-school program called EATWISE (Educated and Aware Teens Who Inspire Smart Eating). Before joining this Park West High School organization, members reported they were addicted to "snack crack"—that is, junk food so named because of the sugar high it provides.[29]

In Teaneck, New Jersey: The Fruit Tree Planting Foundation hopes to plant 18 billion trees around the world. In one of this group's recent projects, seniors at Teaneck High School in New Jersey planted pear, peach, plum, apple, nectarine, and persimmon trees on the grounds of elementary schools.[30]

In Appleton, Wisconsin: Appleton Central Alternative School takes pride in serving kids fresh produce and nonchemically processed foods low in salt, sugar, and fat. Since dietary changes have been implemented, educators say they have proof that students concentrate better; think more clearly; have fewer health complaints, better attendance, and fewer disciplinary referrals; and show a willingness to eat healthier food outside of school.[31]

Intervention from heads of government has been known to make a difference. In 2005, then British prime minister Tony Blair took action after a meeting with chef Jamie Oliver. Oliver, born in Great Britain and now a Food Network host, was alarmed at UK obesity statistics and the quality of school food. The Oliver-Blair meeting ended in establishment of the School Food Trust, which has led to use of healthier ingredients in Great Britain and better training for the people who cook.[32]

Nutritionists and others are hoping it can happen in the United States, too.

NOTES

1. Ann Cooper and Lisa M. Holmes, *Lunch Lessons* (New York: HarperCollins, 2006), xiv–xv.

2. Cooper and Holmes, *Lunch Lessons*, 41.

3. Tara Parker-Pope, "Obama's New Chef Skewers School Lunches," *New York Times* blog, January 29, 2009, 1, well.blogs. nytimes.com/2009/29/new-white-house-chef-skewers-school-lunches/ (accessed February 6, 2009).

4. Lynn Olver, ed., "FAQs: Scholl Lunches," Food Timeline, 1, www.foodtimeline.org/foodschools.html (accessed February 3, 2009).

5. "History of School Lunch," *Chicago Tribune*, November 10, 2008, archives.chicagotribune.com/2008/nov/10/nation/chi-school_ lunch_breakout_boxnov10 (accessed February 3, 2009).

6. "National School Lunch Program," Nebraska Department of Education, 1–2, www.nde.state.ne.us/NS/nslp/overview.htm (accessed February 3, 2009).

7. Alice Waters and Katrina Heron, "No Lunch Left Behind," *New York Times*, February 20, 2009, A31.

8. Winnie Hu, "Too Busy to Eat: Students Get a New Required Course: Lunch," *New York Times*, May 24, 2008, A1, A13.

9. Cari Scribner, "School Lunch Programs Pinched," *Daily Gazette* (Schenectady, NY), August 8, 2008, www.dailygazette.com/ news/2008/aug/08/0808_lunch/ (accessed February 1, 2009).

10. China Millman, "A Call for Obama to Change School Lunch Policy," *Pittsburgh Post-Gazette*, February 8, 2009, www. post-gazette.com/pg/09039/947197–34.stm (accessed February 9, 2009).

11. Quoted in Carol Pogash, "Free Lunch Isn't Cool, So Some Students Go Hungry," *New York Times*, March 1, 2008, www.nytimes.com/2008/03/01/education/01lunch.html?_ r=1&pagewanted=print (accessed February 6, 2009).

12. Alfred Lubrano, "USDA to Kill Phila. School Lunch Program," *Philadelphia Inquirer*, October 22, 2008, findarticles.com/p/articles/ mi_kmtpi/is_200810/ai_n30921087/ (accessed February 1, 2009).

13. Winnie Hu, "As Food Costs Rise, So Do School Lunch Prices," *New York Times*, August 24, 2008, www.nytimes. com/2008/08/25/education/25lunches.html (accessed February 4, 2009).

14. Pogash, "Free Lunch Isn't Cool, So Some Students Go Hungry."

15. Jodie Morse, "Flunking Lunch," *Time*, November 27, 2002, www.time.com/time/magazine/article/0,9171,393733,00.html (accessed February 5, 2009).

16. Nanci Hellmich, "Health Movement Has School Cafeterias in a Food Fight," *USA Today*, www.usatoday.com/news/health/2005–08–21-junk-food-cover_x.htm (accessed February 4, 2009).

17. Martha Mendoza, "Nutrition Class Not Curbing Junk-Food Craving," *Boston Globe*, July 5, 2007, www.boston.com/news/nation/articles/2007/07/05/nutrition_class_not_curbing_junk_food_craving/ (accessed November 15, 2007).

18. Cooper and Holmes, *Lunch Lessons*, 37.

19. Cooper and Holmes, *Lunch Lessons*, 52.

20. Hellmich, "Health Movement Has School Cafeterias in a Food Fight."

21. Cooper and Holmes, *Lunch Lessons*, 58.

22. Patricia Leigh Brown, "Bake Sales Fall Victim to Push for Healthier Foods," *New York Times*, November 10, 2008, www.nytimes.com/2008/11/10/us/10bake.html?_r=1&partner=rss&pagewanted=print (accessed February 9, 2009).

23. Hellmich, "Health Movement Has School Cafeterias in a Food Fight."

24. Hellmich, "Health Movement Has School Cafeterias in a Food Fight."

25. Molly O'Neill, "To a Child, Staff of Life Is Surely Peanut Butter," *New York Times*, August 29, 1990, www.nytimes.com/1990/08/29/garden/to-a-child-staff-of-life-is-surely-peanut-butter.html (accessed March 8, 2008), and Kim Severson, "Who's Sticking with Us?" *New York Times*, February 4, 2009, D1, D5.

26. Brown, "Bake Sales Fall Victim to Push for Healthier Foods."

27. Cooper and Holmes, *Lunch Lessons*, 66–67.

28. Cooper and Holmes, *Lunch Lessons*, 49–50.

29. Cooper and Holmes, *Lunch Lessons*, 54–55.

30. Howard Prosnitz, "Two Orchards Planted in Teaneck to Educate," *Teaneck Suburbanite*, November 26, 2008, 43.

31. Cooper and Holmes, *Lunch Lessons*, 59–60.

32. Lauren Paige Kennedy, "Naked Lunch," *WebMD, the Magazine*, September/October 2008, 78.

10 Eating Out

"There's nothing in the refrigerator!"

"It's your turn to set the table!"

"Do we have to eat *that again?*"

"Forget it. Let's go out."

Does that sound like your family? As of 2008 almost half the money paid out for food annually by Americans was spent in restaurants. Almost one in two Americans eat out on any given day.[1]

This rush on restaurants wasn't always the norm. Ask your parents, or, for sure, your grandparents. Until the last few decades eating out was often considered a rare treat. So what has brought Americans to the point of spending half a trillion dollars a year, in about 925,000 restaurants?[2] The answer lies in the combined effects of more women in the workplace, speeded-up lifestyles, ease of transportation, affordable fast food, new interest in fine dining, and emphasis on food in the media.

PATTERNS OF TEENAGERS

As of 2007, kids and teenagers ate out "more than any other generation—twenty-four times a month," according to a Harris Interactive poll. Pollsters tell us that in addition to spending your own money on food at drive-thrus, convenience stores, and restaurants, you also influence your parents in deciding where to eat out.[3]

"If money were no object, it is likely that my family would eat out more."

—Shelly, age sixteen

Although Alex says he eats out less often than the teen average, when he does eat out, he and his family decide together where to go.

Some restaurants are suspicious of teens in groups. Samara, age sixteen, who eats out often with friends, says, "Usually we're treated like adults, but sometimes waiters, or whoever's working there, keep an eye on us." Vincent, age eighteen, says his friends might "act up a little, like joking around" in a fast-food place, but "if it was a higher class restaurant we would eat with proper manners." Ordinarily, the way to get good service in a restaurant is to take as your models the most mature, considerate patrons.

Even if your behavior is appropriate, restaurant managers may jump to the conclusion that groups of teens will take up a lot of space, not spend much money, and tip badly. Amy, nineteen, who works at a shop known mainly for its ice cream, says that teenagers are just as unpredictable as all other customers and that sometimes they tip really well.

On your part, consider the position of restaurant owners and servers and avoid unreasonable sharing of food and stingy tipping. And at the same time, hope that they treat you with respect, regardless of your age, because that's what hosts should

EATING OUT WITH FRIENDS—WHAT TO DO?

1. Three friends and you, spur of the moment, decide to eat out together. Each has a different idea about where to go. How do you decide?
2. You like your friend and want to eat out with him or her, but this friend isn't worried about cost and you are. How can you resolve this difference gracefully?
3. You're in a restaurant with a couple of friends who are getting negative attention from other diners. They're talking too loudly or misusing cell phones. What do you do?
4. You're eating out with a friend who keeps getting or sending text messages during dinner. You might as well be by yourself. What do you do?
5. You're dissatisfied with what you ordered. Maybe it isn't what you expected, or they didn't prepare it the way you asked. How do you go about registering a complaint?
6. You're with four friends. The bill comes. One kid ordered food that was more expensive. Someone suggests dividing the bill evenly, five ways. What do you think?

do. If restaurant managers treat you well (that is, allow you to sit and talk, or study, without buying much) chances are you'll remember and continue to give them your business when you have even greater spending power.

UNCERTAIN TIMES

Whether the eating-out trend will continue is uncertain. In tough circumstances families usually spend more time cooking. Even though statistics from 2008 suggest that prices went up more for food-eaten-at-home than for food in restaurants,[4] you and your family may find you can save money by eating at home.

HABITS VARY WIDELY

Some families never eat out. In other families, eating at home every night is unthinkable. With 60 percent of mothers working and fast-food chains flourishing, eating out is often worth the price. "Simply put, restaurants are more efficient than you are."[5] Still, even when money is no object, a lot of people prefer eating at home.

EARLIEST RESTAURANTS

Care for some fishballs or pig's head? You could have had some in a *taverna* in ancient Rome. Or, along with everyone else then, including emperors, you could have eaten hot snacks on the street served from outdoor stalls. In colonial America you could have stopped at a "publick house," or inn, where food was available but not known for its tastiness. Restaurants as we know them today originated in France at the end of the 1700s.[6]

The word *restaurant* comes from the French word *restaurer*, meaning "to restore," so that the earliest examples weren't fancy gourmet establishments at all but places that sold meat-based soup to people who weren't feeling well. Restaurants gained in popularity when the French Revolution and Industrial Revolution brought about changes. Chefs who formerly worked for aristocrats needed employment. The rise in importance of the common man meant that ordinary people began to eat out. Industrial advances led to mass production and greater mobility, and now we find ourselves with a range of choices from four-star restaurants to Dunkin' Donuts.[7]

CHOICES NOW

These days, with more than 90,000 restaurants in this country, choosing a restaurant is almost as challenging as cooking a meal. Obviously some decisions are easy—you're in a hurry and have almost no money, so the closest fast food place is where you go. Or, as Alexis, age sixteen, says, "My parents usually make the decision and I don't have much input because I am not paying for it."

DECIDING WHERE TO GO

Do you eat out with friends often or only on special occasions? If you always go to the same familiar places, you probably don't

KINDS OF RESTAURANTS, PAST AND PRESENT[8]

Cafés and coffee houses: In the past and now, coffee houses have served a purpose beyond just selling coffee. Coffee, by the way, was originally considered a medical or religious aid. Starting at the end of the 1400s, coffee's popularity spread from the Muslim world to Europe. Coffee houses in colonial America, beginning in the 1700s, were often places to share news, conduct business, and hold discussions.

Delicatessens: The German word means "delicacies," and until the late 1800s most American delicatessens were run by Germans. These stores sold sandwiches, cooked meats, and canned and prepared foods. Eventually Jewish Americans opened delis, featuring such typical items as smoked fish, corned beef, potato knishes, and pickles. Although many delicatessens are kosher, delis may be run by any ethnic group.

Automats: From 1902 until 1991 Americans in certain big cities had access to Horn & Hardart, described as "waiterless lunchrooms," which offered tasty food at low cost. Diners put nickels into slots and out popped hot and cold food. Especially popular in the Depression and World War II, Horn & Hardart went bankrupt when American eating habits changed.

Fast-food restaurants: The concept of fast food may have been known as early as 1848, but common use of the term dates from the 1960s in the United States, when chain restaurants took off. McDonald's, originating in California, was the first to use an assembly-line system, but White Castle, founded in Wichita, Kansas, actually preceded it.

have to make many decisions. But if you want to break out of the usual, or you need to be in an unfamiliar neighborhood, how do you decide where to go?

Let's assume your friends are energetic, adventurous, flexible, and not completely broke. They're ready and willing—but leaving the dining choice up to you. You can prepare ahead of time by consulting

1. the Yellow Pages of local phone books; Yellow Pages may include actual menus.

2. ads in local newsletters, newspapers, and magazines that may offer discount coupons and/or restaurant reviews.

3. restaurant guides, in book form; eating guides for various cities—such as Zagat, Michelin, Fodor, and Frommer—evaluate all aspects of restaurants, including quality, cost, ambience, and service. Some focus on well-known, expensive restaurants and others on everyday, casual eating.

4. endless information on the Internet. Type your requirements into a search engine—"inexpensive Italian restaurant," for instance—in a general location, and if you're searching a busy commercial area you'll probably find what you need.

MENU, PLEASE

At the earliest taverns and inns a set menu was offered to everyone. Eaters and food arrived at the table at the same time, with no room for choice. Starting in the 1700s, however, printed menus appeared. Now guests could read descriptions of unseen dishes, make personal selections, and know in advance how much food would cost.

The English word *menu*, by the way, was borrowed from French by way of the Latin *minutus*, meaning "detailed list." Children's menus, said to have originated in the United States in the 1930s, were developed by railroad companies in an attempt to cater to kids of traveling parents.[9]

If all this preplanning seems unnecessary and time-consuming, you can always walk up and down the streets, or the mall, to size up restaurants for yourself. Many will have menus (with prices) posted near the entrance. Almost all will be happy to show you a menu before you commit yourself. The size and appearance of the restaurant, outside and inside, will give you clues about cuisine, type of service, and cost.

If you eat out regularly you'll gradually get to know the scene. At some places you'll need a reservation, especially on weekends or in large groups. Other places, though crowded, may not take reservations. Their logic is that biggest profits are made from constant turnover of tables. Besides that, owners may decide that a waiting line makes the restaurant look popular.

If you're thinking that reservations and restaurant reviews are only for special occasions, think again. Most restaurant guides and reviews want to be friendly to ordinary eaters. The Zagat Survey, started in 1979, publishes ratings sent in by volunteers. Although it originally covered New York City restaurants only, Zagat has branched out to more than seventy cities.[10] These guides, updated every year, use a 30-point scale to rate restaurants on food, décor, service, and cost. They also include descriptions from individual diners, such as "tasty and filling dumplings," "granddaddy of steakhouses," and "dull décor and haphazard service."

FOUR-STAR RESTAURANTS— WHAT'S THE BIG DEAL?

We've already mentioned celebrity chefs and world-famous restaurants. Nice for those who can afford them. So what's the difference between a decent meal and a multi-star dining experience, and why are some willing to spend on one dinner as much as others spend on food for a week or two? Maybe you'd like the world's best car someday. And your friend wants the coolest wardrobe. Still others dream of the best meal in the world's best restaurant. Tastes differ.

ARE FOODIES BORN OR MADE?

Although chef Anthony Bourdain, as a child, had the good luck to be taken by ship to Europe, many chefs and gourmet cooks haven't had the benefit of privileged childhoods. Some food lovers can't explain where their interest and appreciation came from, and others believe they learned from early experiences.

Some Kids Are Getting an Early Start

According to journalist Alexandra Zissu, there's a "growing wave of parents obsessed with all things culinary who are indoctrinating their children to the ways of gastronomy. For these children peanut butter and jelly sandwiches and mac and cheese are no longer standard fare. They prefer ethnic and gourmet goods. . . . Chicken fingers are lost on this crowd."[11]

Zissu reports further evidence that certain kids—possibly city kids, surely privileged kids—are learning more than ever these days about good food. Toy companies say they're getting more requests for pretend cookware and food. Some youngsters prefer the Food Network to the Cartoon Network. And Chef Mario Batali says he sees plenty of young people at his exceptional, expensive restaurants.

Zissu adds, "Parents seeking to tantalize their offspring's taste buds are usually foodies themselves. Some mothers start children's gastronomic education while still pregnant, eating spicy and garlicky meals, and continue to do so while nursing, citing research that suggests children exposed to many tastes through breast milk or in the womb are less likely to be picky eaters."[12]

David Kamp is a parent who wants his kids to enjoy good food as soon as possible. "Discovering new foods and flavors is one of the most delightful experiences that childhood can offer," he says. "Personally, I far preferred it to reading and exercising. It pains me," he continues, "that many children now grow up eating little besides golden-brown logs of kid food, especially in a time when the quality, variety and availability of good ingredients is better than ever." Although kids' menus are a comfort to many restaurant goers, Kamp sees them as money-driven gimmicks for owners and easy outs for parents.[13]

Food Prodigy

Most kids left alone at dinnertime would, at best, thaw out a frozen dinner. But not David Fishman of New York City, who wants to be a food critic some day. In 2008 twelve-year-old David got media attention for eating out—alone—at a new Italian restaurant that caught his fancy. He ordered their specialty, prosciutto (Italian smoked ham); sampled a complimentary tripe stew (intestines); met the chef; went home with a sample of hazelnut spread; and took notes on his meal. About the tripe stew he said, "It wasn't my favorite."[14]

David at age six, by the way, won a competition for best new cupcake concept. Meanwhile David's extraordinary interest in food is said to be the concept for movie about a kid like him.[15]

WHO NEEDS AN EXPENSIVE RESTAURANT?

Frequent dining in expensive restaurants is out of reach for most teenagers. You may never be willing to splurge, especially when good affordable food can be found. And let's be clear. "Expensive" doesn't necessarily mean excellent. In popular and trafficked locations (resorts, tourist sites, and airports) inflated prices may not be indictors of quality. You may be paying for proximity to a ski lift or tourist attraction rather than for great food.

Nevertheless, some restaurants have reason to be expensive. Notable chefs command high salaries, their support staffs are large, ingredients are costly, and overhead expenses are high. Diners go there expecting dishes almost impossible to imitate, served lavishly, in a setting that's attractive and comfortable. If you get the chance to go to one, are you going to pass it up?

When Brooke and Rebecca, two high school–age culinary arts students were taken as a special treat to Le Bernardin, a four-star restaurant, their first reaction was that "it looks

> ### 🍴 "ONE OF THE BEST MEALS I EVER HAD"
>
> *A few summers ago Caitlin Leibenhaut, now eighteen, was on vacation with her family in the south of Spain.*
>
> We were wandering about the town, trying to find a decent spot to eat, when we stumbled on this small complex with multiple restaurants. All within the same area there was a Chinese restaurant, an English pub, and what seemed to be a very upscale restaurant.
>
> Seeing that we were in Spain, the Chinese restaurant didn't seem like the best idea. The English pub didn't have much variety, so we decided to treat ourselves to an expensive meal. It turned out that this restaurant was brand new and not as expensive as we had originally thought.
>
> We ended up being the only customers there, had the full attention of the entire wait staff, and were given little extras (intermezzos). It was one of the best meals I ever had in my life. It is still my memory of the best steak, and every steak I eat is now compared to *this* steak, at this random restaurant in the south of Spain.

like somewhere Donald Trump would eat." Even though Le Bernardin seemed like another world to them, as chefs-in-training they began to appreciate "the attention to detail," "the way sauce was poured over a slice of fish tableside," and the way the restaurant makes "everyone feel like they're special and the service is just for you."[16]

On the other hand, humorist David Sedaris, like a lot of people, says that fine restaurants are wasted on him because he can't tell the difference between a peach and an apricot, let alone an excellent truffle and a mediocre one. Furthermore, as a "shoveller, a quantity man," he doesn't appreciate the notion that the more expensive the restaurant, the smaller the portions.[17]

HOW DO YOU KNOW WHAT TO ORDER?

Whether prices are rock-bottom or astronomical, before you go to a new-to-you restaurant find out what it's noted for. Even your local diner is better at one thing than another. Restaurants often label themselves by specialty or cuisine, for example, steak, fish, vegetarian, Southern, French, or Thai. It's smart to go with what they claim they do best. And why not wait to have seafood until you're near the ocean, rather than ordering it in the middle of Kansas? On the other hand, in these days of global living, almost anything can be shipped safely anywhere, so if a restaurant is reliable, order whatever you want and can afford.

Servers may try to lure you with descriptions of specials. It's usually smart to ask prices if they don't announce them. It's also fine to ask servers questions about menu items and to make reasonable requests concerning your personal preferences. A server's opinion may be helpful. They themselves have often tasted menu items and heard reactions from other customers, and it's in their interests to make you happy with your order.

FOOD SAFETY IN RESTAURANTS

Dining out isn't always a pleasure. About 40 percent of reported food-borne disease can be traced to commercial food establishments.[18] When you're eating out you'd like to think you're at least as safe as at home. In order to protect diners, restaurants in the United States are regularly inspected by local, county, or state health department personnel. Health inspectors, rating restaurants on the basis of a perfect score of 100, make deductions if they find food kept at the wrong temperature, if uncertified equipment is used, and if infestations of vermin are found. Infractions lead to citations and then to fines for offenders.

Occasionally inspectors will close a place down. A certificate of health should be posted in the restaurant, and you can also go on line to check its status. To find the appropriate website for your area, click on www.allfoodbusiness.com/health_inspections.php.

CALORIE COUNTS

Do you eat more, and more fattening things, when you go to a restaurant? Because eating out is thought to be contributing

177

to obesity, U.S. restaurants are being pressured to provide nutrition information. The amount of pressure varies from one area to another, but chain restaurants are more and more frequently posting calorie counts. New York City has taken the lead in requiring restaurants with fifteen or more locations to give calorie information on the menu, rather than merely on websites, tray liners, or placards at the register.[19] Chains that don't provide calorie information risk having to pay expensive penalties.

Predictably, restaurants don't like telling customers that a monster cheeseburger is 1,500–1,700 calories and a thirty-two-ounce triple-thick chocolate milkshake is 1,160. The good news for nutritionists, however, is that a lot of restaurants, because of customer demands, are taking initiative themselves. Starbucks, for example, claims to have saved the nation 17 billion calories in one year by replacing whole milk with 2 percent milk.[20]

IF YOU LIKE RESTAURANTS, WORK IN ONE

One way to get into the best restaurant is to work there. Culinary training is becoming more and more popular, available, and practical. Irena Chalmers, author of *Food Jobs: 150 Great Jobs for Culinary Students, Career Changers and Food Lovers*, urges food-career seekers to follow their specific interests. For instance, a teenage student of Chalmers who loved to shop found a career as a tabletop consultant—someone responsible for choosing china and glassware in upscale restaurants. Another student of hers, whose cooking skills exceeded his English language ability, found work as a chef at the Korean Embassy in Washington, DC.

In addition to jobs involving actual food preparation Chalmers' book lists related occupations, such as food writer, food-shop owner, bartender, food photographer, recipe tester, and cooking-school teacher.[21] Remember that no matter which way the economy goes, people have to eat.

JOBS IN FAST FOOD

Teenagers have traditionally found part-time work in fast-food restaurants, which often hire people with little or no experience. When times are good, many middle-class students may not work at all, or may hold out for jobs that pay better or provide more prestige than fast-food jobs. Kids who do work at fast-food outlets sometimes feel, as sixteen-year-old Dave Neuzil does, that "it's not considered cool, working at a fast-food place. [Other kids'] parents just give them everything. But I need to make some money." Confirming these snobbish teenage attitudes, manager Jim LaRose finds that certain high school–age customers who come into his Subway are "very arrogant."[22]

But in tougher economic times teens may not be in a position to turn up their noses at fast-food jobs—jobs that provide not only income but experience. Aside from learning how to be responsible, to work with a team, and to deal with customers—skills you might learn on any job—specific training in food service may set you up for advancement. If you're looking for a fast-food job, it's smart to find an employer who provides the following benefits: paid job training, mentoring, reasonable hours, chances for advancement, and incentives such as scholarships.

Although we don't usually think of fast-food employment as a fast track to fame, some chains have developed incentives more attention-getting than scholarships. Since 2006 McDonald's has sought the good will of their employees—and publicity for themselves—by sponsoring a worldwide singing competition. The employee who wins the Voice of McDonald's contest gets special attention and a $25,000 prize.[23]

Going to restaurants is one of the best ways to expand your food horizons. Experimentation can be fun. Young adults reputedly consume one-third less ethnic food than the average adult,[24] but why not lead the pack to an unusual restaurant? Eating out is a great adventure if you can afford it, so stimulate the economy—and your taste buds—by doing it when you can.

CHECK YOUR RESTAURANT IQ

1. If you want *smorgasbord*, you'll go to
   a. a Swiss restaurant
   b. a buffet that offers various hot and cold dishes
   c. an all-you-can-eat restaurant
2. Ordering *a la carte* means ordering
   a. separate items from the menu at separate prices
   b. a set meal with several courses, all at one price
   c. a meal with dessert included
3. If you choose an *entrée*, you're choosing
   a. a pre-dinner, or appetizer, course
   b. a piece of meat
   c. the main course of a meal
4. If you ask for pasta *al dente*, you want it
   a. served without tomato sauce
   b. cooked so that it's soft
   c. cooked so that it's firm
5. If you go for *dim sum*, you'll choose
   a. small pieces of raw fish
   b. small filled dumplings
   c. small sweet cakes
6. If a soup or sauce is a *puree*, it
   a. has no artificial ingredients
   b. has been made smooth in a food processor
   c. has a base of chicken broth
7. If you order *steak tartare*, you'll get
   a. beef with a peppery sauce
   b. a rare hamburger
   c. raw chopped beef
8. If you order *venison*, you'll get the meat of
   a. a deer
   b. a wild boar
   c. an ostrich
9. If you order an *enchilada*, you'll get
   a. an omelet with spicy sauce
   b. a rolled corn pancake with filling
   c. a very hot pepper
10. A *fillet* (*filet*) of meat or fish means
    a. the most expensive cut or part
    b. it's stuffed
    c. bones have been removed

Answers: 1. b; 2. a; 3. c; 4. c; 5. b; 6. b; 7. c; 8. a; 9. b; 10. c

NOTES

1. Ben Steverman, "Lean Time for Restaurants," BusinessWeek, www.businessweek.com/nvestor/content/apr2008/pi2008047_931670_page_2.htm (accessed February 4, 2010).

2. "Is Eating Out Cheaper Than Cooking?" *Christian Science Monitor*, 1, articles.moneycentral.msn.com/SavingandDebt/SaveMoney/IsEatingOutCheaperThanCooking.aspx (accessed March 7, 2009).

3. Derek Gale, "Purchasing Power of Kids and Teens," Restaurants & Institutions, February 1, 2007, www.rimag.com/article/CA6521391.html (accessed March 5, 2009).

4. Annette Clauson, "Despite Higher Food Prices, Percent of U.S. Income Spent on Food Remains Constant," *Amber Waves*, September 2008, www.ers.usda.gov/AmberWaves/September08/Findings/PercentofIncome.htm (accessed March 7, 2009).

5. Clauson, "Despite Higher Food Prices," 2.

6. Lynn Olver, "FAQs: Restaurants, Chefs, & Foodservice," Food Timeline, 1, 25, www.foodtimeline.org/restaurants.html (accessed March 9, 2009).

7. Olver, "FAQs: Restaurants, Chefs, & Foodservice," 2 , 4.

8. Olver, "FAQs: Restaurants, Chefs, & Foodservice, 10–12, 23–24.

9. Olver, "FAQs: Restaurants, Chefs, & Foodservice," 1, 25.

10. "Zagat Survey," Wikipedia, en.wikipedia.org/wiki/Zagat (accessed March 16, 2009).

11. Alexandra Zissu, "These Kids Never Say 'Yech!'" *New York Times*, January 28, 2007.

12. Zissu, "These Kids Never Say 'Yech!'" ST6.

13. David Kamp, "Don't Point That Menu at My Child, Please," *New York Times*, May 30, 2007, F1, F8.

14. Susan Dominus, "12-Year-Old's a Food Critic, and the Chef Loves It," *New York Times*, November 17, 2008, A23.

15. Dominus, "12-Year-Old's a Food Critic, and the Chef Loves It," A23.

16. Kim Severson, "Two Students, Four Stars," Reblog from *New York Times*, www.hastac.org/node/750 (accessed February 21, 2009).

17. David Sedaris, "Tasteless," *New Yorker*, September 3 and 10, 2007, 98.

18. Timothy F. Jones, Boris I. Pavlin, Bonnie J. LaFleur, L Amanda Ingram, and Willian Schaffner, "Restaurant Inspection

Scores and Foodborne Disease," CDC, April 2004, www.cdc.gov/ncidod/EID/vol10no4/03–0343.htm (accessed March 19, 2009).

19. James Barron, "5 Restaurants in Manhattan Get Citations Over Calories," *New York Times*, May 6, 2008, www.nytimes.com/2008/05/06/nyregion/06calorie.html (accessed February 21, 2009).

20. Kim Severson, "Calories Do Count," *New York Times*, October 29, 2008, D1.

21. Irena Chalmers, *Food Jobs: 150 Great Jobs for Culinary Students, Career Changers and Food Lovers* (New York: Beaufort Books, 2008), 1–2.

22. Dirk Johnson, "For Teenagers, Fast Food Is a Snack, Not a Job," *New York Times*, January 8, 2001, 1, www.nytimes.com/2001/01/08/us/for-teenagers-fast-food-is-a-snack-not-a-job.html (accessed April 5, 2009).

23. Andrew Martin, "McDonald's Is Looking for Musical Talent Behind Its Counters," *New York Times*, February 9, 2008, C1.

24. "Insights into Tomorrow's Ethnic Food & Drink Consumers," the-infoshop.com, www.the-infoshop.com/study/dc32475-ethnic-food_toc.html (accessed April 6, 2009).

11 Going to Extremes

Don't starve yourself. Don't stuff yourself. Eat in moderation. This advice is often given and often ignored. Clayton, age sixteen, says that in his

> freshman year of high school I joined the wrestling team. In wrestling you can barely eat a thing, because week after week you have to maintain your lowest possible body weight. I wanted to lose weight not only for wrestling but for my health. But after wrestling was over and I lost all the necessary weight, it just seemed less and less important to fast.
>
> So, the day after the last meet, a couple of guys and I went to a local stand and had a competition to see who could eat the most slider-style burgers. I could only finish an abysmal eight, while my friend doubled my effort at 16. I may not have been the winner, but the stomach ache I had afterward certainly made me feel I did the best I could.

Indian leader Mahatma Gandhi sometimes ate nothing. In his lifetime he went on seventeen hunger strikes, existing on water alone, in some cases for more than two weeks at a time. At the other extreme, competitive eater Joey Chestnut consumed sixty-six hot dogs and buns in twelve minutes. Let's forget moderation for the moment and examine extremes of famine and feast.

183

FASTING

When almost 35,000 people around the world die tragically every day because of not getting enough food,[1] why would anyone choose *not* to eat? People who fast—that is, willingly abstain from eating, drinking, or both, for a period of time—usually do it for one of the following reasons: (1) religious or spiritual, (2) medical, (3) health or sports related, (4) political, or (5) as a stunt.

Religious Fasts

Do you ever give up food temporarily in connection with your religion? Most religions urge limited fasting as an act of faith or penitence. Muslims, for example, are expected to fast all the daytime hours during the month of Ramadan; Hindus may fast weekly, monthly, or during festivals. Christians may give up a particular food for the forty days of Lent before Easter, and observant Jews refrain from eating on Yom Kippur, or the Day of Atonement, and on Tisha B'Av. Aside from these examples of prescribed religious fasts, some people claim to find a kind of spiritual enlightenment when they go without food.

Medical Fasts

In certain medical situations—blood or cholesterol-level tests—you need to fast for some hours before testing. Or, like young teenager Greta Koch, you'll fast before surgery, since food in the system can cause problems with anesthesia. "I wasn't allowed to eat for a day and a half," Greta says. "It was one of the hardest things I have ever done. At the end, my stomach was pleading with me to eat something. I also got a lot of cravings during that day and a half, like Chinese, Mexican, and chocolate—none of the healthy foods I usually eat. When I recovered, I made my mom take me out for a big plate of Chinese noodles."

Fasts for Weight Loss and Health

Therapeutic fasting, that is, not eating in order to lose weight or to improve health, is a controversial practice. When you fast your body uses up stored energy, which is why you lose weight. Because of metabolic changes in your body caused by fasting, however, it's doubtful whether that weight will stay off permanently.[2] Fasting on alternate days may help people lose weight, even if they eat more than usual on nonfasting days, but again, research indicates that these dieters can't maintain their lower weight.[3]

Teenagers involved in sports sometimes fast on a limited basis in order to gain an advantage by coming in at a certain weight. After competition ends, these athletes usually bounce back immediately—or gain extra.

Once in a while fasting leads to permanent weight loss, as in the case of a 456-pound Scottish man (known as Mr. A. B., age twenty-seven). Under the care of physicians, existing on water and supplements only, he went 382 days without food, reduced to 276 pounds, and after five years gained back only 16.[4]

Green Vegetable Juice?

Maybe you've heard adults talk about going to a fasting spa—usually an expensive retreat where they're pampered and seriously deprived of most food. In writer Judith Thurman's three-day stay at a California spa, for instance, she lost a pound a day and left "squeaky clean inside and out, with bright eyes, a flat stomach, and skin like a rose petal." Bad news was that a week later she was back at her old weight.[5]

Cleaning Yourself Out

What about cleansing your bodies of impurities by skipping food, or eating only raw foods for a day or two and drinking nothing but water, a little juice, or tea? Although studies in both rodents and humans show that fasting might delay the onset of diseases such as Alzheimer's, heart disease, and diabetes, there's no evidence that fasting detoxifies the body. Most scientists say that fasting isn't necessary, since the skin, liver, colon, and kidneys are designed to remove toxins.[6] Still, many people who fast claim they feel better after the experience.

Fasting to Make a Point

"I won't eat until you meet my demands!" Ever try that? In the case of Mahatma Gandhi, for instance, fasting was intended to protest a wrong or bring awareness to a cause. Gandhi, a vegetarian, fasted both to purify himself and to protest actions that kept his native India from becoming independent.

Sometimes groups, rather than individuals, conduct hunger strikes. Although it's easy to dismiss the effectiveness of hunger strikes, this form of nonviolent protest has sometimes brought about change. For instance, British and U.S. women suffragettes fasted as part of their efforts to get the vote for women. You could, yourself, get an idea what a hunger strike might be like by going along with projects sponsored by organizations such as Oxfam. Oxfam asks you to give up eating for one day and to donate the money you saved to the relief of world hunger.

Fasting as a Competitive Stunt

If you can't imagine fasting at all, you'll probably think Giovanni Succi's stunts were ridiculous. In the 1800s he fasted more than thirty times before audiences in the capitals of Europe. Believing himself possessed with a spirit that allowed him to live without food, he went without it for as long as forty-five days. Between shows he was regularly admitted to an insane asylum.[7]

In 2003, when magician David Blaine lived without food in a six-foot-long box, strung up in the air in London for forty-four days, audience reaction was mixed. "Some women held banners declaring their love and support. Others ran naked under the box. Some men said David Blaine was a hero. Some called him an idiot."[8]

Would you have been turned off by his stunt? Some people found it so distasteful that they pelted Blaine's box with rotten eggs. And yet, when he came out of his box after forty-four days, Blaine claimed he had learned to appreciate simple things more in this "most important experience of his life."[9]

Pathological Fasting

Fasting for a short time in the name of religion, health, or politics is considered to be rational and maybe even noble. Refusal to eat at all is quite another matter. Anorexia nervosa, mentioned briefly in chapter 4, is an eating disorder characterized by extremely low body weight, as a result of rejecting most food. The anorexic (often, but not always, a teenager girl) wrongly believes that she, or he, is overweight. Anorexia is obviously a serious disorder that should be managed by experienced professionals.

EATING OUTSIDE THE BOX

Some people clearly eat too little or two much. Others go to extremes in terms of the unusualness of what they eat. Necessity sometimes demands a limited or odd diet, as in, if you're lost in the woods you make do with berries and nuts. Or else you enjoy experimentation, as in, yes, let me try that rattlesnake meat.

Unusual Eating by Necessity

Maybe you've bought freeze-dried foods and trail mix as substitutes for heavier supplies on a camping trip. Or maybe you've sampled freeze-dried ice cream or some other novelty inspired by the needs of astronauts. Just as long voyages in the past required food adaptations (citrus fruits on ships, to prevent scurvy) trips in space also call for adaptations. Food has to be (1) nutritious, easily digestible, and palatable; (2) engineered for consumption in a zero-gravity environment; (3) light, well-packaged, quick to serve, easy to clean up; and (4) easy to store and to open, leaving little waste.

HOW DO ASTRONAUTS EAT?[10]

Can you swallow normally in space?

Experts were originally concerned about swallowing in weightless conditions, but John Glenn, the first American to orbit Earth in 1962, had no difficulties.

Early on, how was food packaged?

The food of Project Gemini (1965–1966) improved on the food of Project Mercury (1959–1963) by eliminating tubes heavier than the food they contained and by adding gelatin coating to help prevent crumbling.

How have astronauts dealt with limitations?

Astronauts were mildly rebuked for sneaking a corned beef sandwich onto a spaceflight. It was feared that floating pieces of bread might pose a problem.

Has astronaut dining improved?

By the time of Skylab (1973–1974), on-board refrigerator and freezer became possible, plus table and chair fastened to the floor. These days, astronauts eat fresh fruits and vegetables and can request personalized menus.

What do astronauts drink?

Various rehydratable drinks. Carbonated drinks aren't favored in space because of irregularities in burping caused by microgravity.

Germinated Chick Peas and Wheatgrass Juice[11]

Astronauts may be restricted but most of us have endless choices. Given all those choices, can you see yourself voluntarily eating only raw food? If you like the idea, you'd probably feel right at home at the Hippocrates Health Food Institute in West Palm Beach, Florida, where you would start the day with a twelve-ounce glass of sunflower green sprout juice. The rest of the day you'd eat 75 percent raw food. You wouldn't be totally deprived, though. The remaining percentage of your day's diet could be foods such as pizza, made with a rice crust, or cheese made from soy, or a tofu burger.

Within the raw-food movement, by the way, are splinter groups—fruitarians only eat fruits with seeds and sproutarians only eat, you guessed it, sprouts.

What's the Logic of a Raw-Food Diet?

Raw-food eaters say cooking destroys or reduces nutrients, vitamins, and enzymes, whereas raw foods contain more of those things, plus fiber. Eating raw also means avoiding chemically altered and processed food. Want to go one step further? Eat *live* food only—if you can catch it fast enough. Believers claim live food gives you more energy, improves your complexion, and cures cancer.[12]

Not everybody is ready to promote raw-food diets. Columbia University director of nutrition Wahida Karmally finds no research to show that a raw diet is healthier than a traditional diet. American Dietetic Association spokesperson JoAnn Hattner adds that since raw food is low in calories, you'll probably lose weight on such as diet, but, for general nutrition, you must move into a raw diet gradually and be very well educated about what you're doing.[13] If you do choose a raw-food diet, you can find support from Internet groups and a few raw food restaurants, primarily in New York and California.

Cooked, but Weird

Most raw food is at least recognizable. If you're eating raw cauliflower, you know it. Some food adventurers, however, specialize in tasting foods that the rest of us can't identify. Thanks to the Discovery Channel we've seen travelers eat pickled snake head or fried creepy crawlers. And we have reports from noted writers such as John McPhee. Writing in 2007 about a recent trip to Alaska, McPhee says, "The moose was tough. I ate little of it. The grizzly was tender with youth and from a winter in the den. More flavorful than any wild meat I have eaten, it expanded my life list—muskrat, weasel, deer, moose, musk ox, Dall sheep, whale, lion, coachwhip, rattlesnake . . . grizzly."[14]

Snake marinated in wine isn't considered unusual in some parts of the world.

Grasshopper Tacos

What's the strangest thing you've ever tasted? Some adventurous eaters want to learn about other cultures. Most are interested in food in general. Certain other are interested in novelty, attention, and bragging rights. Blogger Justin Glow says, "Half the fun of traveling is getting out and enjoying all sorts of foods you're not used to eating. A simple trip to the corner market or grocery store in a foreign land can keep you amused for hours."[15] Among the photographs on his website are salmon candy from San Francisco; canned giant water bugs found in Raleigh, North Carolina; hamburger haw (whatever that is) from Beijing; black bean cheese; and cow lung.

HOW EXCESSIVE CAN YOU GET?

Long before *The Guinness Book of World Records* appeared, humans were competing in every category. Who can run the fastest mile? Who can throw the biggest banquet? The ancient Romans—the rich ones, that is—were famous for their eating orgies, and, in the 1500s, King Henry VIII of England was known for his gluttony. The menu for one of his banquets included 17 pigs, 11 cows, 540 chickens, 6 cranes, 72 geese, 384 pigeons, 648 larks, and 4 peacocks. And then came dessert.[16]

More Than a Piece of Cake

What comes after the banquet? The world's biggest wedding cake, made in 2004 for the New England Bridal Shower Showcase by pastry chef Lynn Mansel and fifty-seven helpers. Seven tiers, seventeen feet high, and weighing 15,032 pounds, it was made from 10,000 pounds of batter, covered with 4,810 pounds of icing and was said to be enough to feed 59,000 people.[17] Meanwhile Chinese creators got into the *Guinness Book of World Records* in 2006 for making an ice cream cake that weighed eight tons.[18]

I CAN EAT MORE THAN YOU CAN!

Do you like pigging out at an all-you-can-eat buffet? No matter how much you can manage to consume, Takeru Kobayashi and Richard LeFevre are in a whole other league. They're among a group of eighteen-and-overs who travel, on a regular basis, to compete in eating contests. At the big one—Nathan's Hot Dogs in Coney Island, New York—and at the approximately 100 other contest locations, competitors see who can down the most chicken wings, glazed doughnuts, or lobsters—all for a very little money and fame.

Why would anyone cram down six pounds of Spam, sixty-five hard boiled eggs, or seven quarter-pound sticks of butter in a few minutes? That's what Harvard Medical School's George

> ## COMPETING FOR THE MUSTARD YELLOW BELT[19]
>
> *When did eating contests begin?*
>
> Thousands of years ago. The founders of the IFOCE—International Federation of Competitive Eating—say that the first competitors were "30 hungry Neanderthals in a cave fighting over a rabbit."
>
> *When was the IFOCE started, and what do they do?*
>
> American brothers George and Richard Shea founded the IFOCE in 1997 in order to develop, promote, and run more than 100 eating events annually. They also produce television shows featuring competitive eating.
>
> *What are some eating contest records?*
>
> In 2007 American Joey Chestnut won the coveted Mustard Yellow Belt by consuming sixty-six Nathan's hot dogs in twelve minutes. Chestnut also holds a pizza-eating record—forty-five slices in ten minutes. Other IFOCE heroes are Takeru Kobayashi—fifty-seven cow brains in fifteen minutes—and Sonya Thomas, who ate eighty chicken nuggets in five minutes.
>
> *What are some of the rules?*
>
> (1) You must be eighteen to enter. (2) Food is weighed or divided into uniform pieces. (3) No one begins until a signal, and food in your mouth at the end counts as eaten. (4) Competitors may drink water during the contest. (5) Anyone who suffers a "Roman incident" (vomiting) is disqualified if the result touches plate or table.
>
> *What do you win?*
>
> Prizes vary from nothing but a title to a few thousand dollars. Sometimes sponsors donate prizes and/or pay travel expenses of competitors.

Blackburn wonders about this "sick, abnormal behavior." Other critics of competitive eating in America and abroad refer to it as "a sport for our degraded times" and a sign of "societal decay."[20]

On the other hand, prominent food researcher Paul Rozin sees such eating as "this great lark" that combines Americans' love of food with their passion for competitive sports. About the competitors—"What a crazy species," he says.[21]

Who *Are* These Competitors?

Competitive eaters are generally, but not always, males. They usually have day jobs and eat competitively as others might take up a sport. Like many athletes, they like the excitement, attention, and traveling. Some are overweight or obese, but at the other end of the spectrum is Sonya Thomas, weighing a mere 100 pounds. According to Jason Fagone, in his book *Horsemen of the Esophagus*, "The eaters weren't staying up nights wondering if they could extract meaning from the grotesque. Eating wasn't grotesque, it was cool, and if the eaters did stay up nights, it was to trade stomach-stretching techniques on the phone or check the latest eating gossip."[22]

FINDING THE RIGHT BALANCE

If you're healthy and well-nourished you can survive without food for about eight weeks, as long as you have water.[23] At the other end of the spectrum, with training and will, you can manage to consume eleven pounds of cheesecake in nine minutes or thirteen pounds of watermelon in fifteen minutes, as others have done.[24] Most of us, however, prefer to avoid extremes in favor of savoring the taste of each bite.

NOTES

1. James Vernon, *Hunger: A Modern History* (Cambridge, MA: Harvard University Press, 2007), 1.

2. "Fasting," WebMD, www.webmd.com/diet/fasting (accessed April 8, 2009).

3. "Fasting."

4. Sharman Apt Russell, *Hunger: An Unnatural History* (New York: Basic Books, 2005), 7–8.

5. Judith Thurman, "The Fast Lane," *New Yorker*, September 3 and 10, 2007, 72–78.

6. Thurman, "The Fast Lane," 72–78.

7. Russell, *Hunger*, 4.

8. Russell, *Hunger*, 6–7.

9. Russell, *Hunger*, 6–7

10. "Space Food," Wikipedia, en.wikipedia.org/wiki/Space_food (accessed May 14, 2009).

11. "Extreme Eating: Raw Foods Diet Takes Healthful Eating to the Edge," *Newsday*, June 10, 1998, www.living-foods.com/news/extreme.html (accessed April 7, 2009).

12. "Extreme Eating."

13. "Extreme Eating."

14. John McPhee, "My Life List," *New Yorker*, September 3 and 10, 2007, 82.

15. Justin Glow, "The Weird Things People Eat around the World," Gadling, June 21, 2007, www.gadling.com/2007/06/21/the-weird-things-people-eat-around-the-world/ (accessed April 8, 2009).

16. *Extreme Gluttons* (Farmington Hills, MI: Blackbirch Press, 2005), 11.

17. "World's Largest Wedding Cake," The Longest List of the Longest Stuff at the Longest Domain Name at Long Last, thelongestlistofthelongeststuffatthelongestdomainnameatlonglast.com/largest70.html (accessed April 6, 2009).

18. "World's Largest Ice Cream Cake," Reuters, January 17, 2006, www.chinadaily.com.cn/english/doc/2006-01/17/content_512867.htm (accessed April 15, 2009).

19. Ed Grabianowski, "How Competitive Eating Works," HowStuffWorks, people.howstuffworks.com/competitive-eating.htm/printable (accessed April 7, 2009).

20. Jason Fagone, *Horsemen of the Esophagus* (New York: Crown, 2006), 12.

21. Fagone, *Horsemen of the Esophagus*, 103.

22. Fagone, *Horsemen of the Esophagus*, 22.

23. Charles Bryant, "How Long Can You Go without Food and Water?" HowStuffWorks, health.howstuffworks.com/live-without-food-and-water1.htm (accessed August 3, 2009).

24. Grabianowski, "How Competitive Eating Works."

12 Eating around the World

Are you more alike or more different, compared to the other 6 billion eaters in the world? There's no easy answer. On the one hand, since most foods can be safely transported over great distances, diets these days may be similar.

To prove that point, Joel Stein, in *Time* magazine, describes a dinner he prepared to show the flip side of the local-food movement. His rule was that ingredients *must* come from a distance of at least 3,000 miles from his Los Angeles home. (The fish came from an island off Argentina, the olive oil from Italy, a coconut from Thailand.)[1] If we're looking for more evidence of the one-world-of-eaters theory, think about Belgians, Australians, and Chinese all eating Big Macs.

On the other hand, differences remain. The Aboubakar family in Darfur province, Sudan, exists each week on a diet of sorghum (a grain), dried goat meat, dried beans, and a few condiments, all of which come to, in U.S. money, $1.23.[2] Their limited supply of water is provided by the Oxfam organization. You can be sure the Aboubakars aren't spending time worrying about whether to eat local or nonlocal food.

IRONY OF MODERN NUTRITION

These days you don't have to travel far to enjoy excellent, authentic specialties. You can get almost the same meals in Austin, Baltimore, or Chicago as in Acapulco, Mexico; Beijing, China; or Cannes, France. The great irony of modern nutrition is that "at a time when hundreds of millions of people do not have

195

WHAT FAMILIES EAT AROUND THE WORLD[3]

In the book *Hungry Planet* thirty families are pictured surrounded by their typical week's food supply. Below are examples of five diets and the cost in American dollars.

The Costa family in *Havana, Cuba*, eats rationed amounts of malanga (potato-like vegetable), bread, rice; yogurt, cheese; small amount of meat, fruit, vegetables; sugar, chili peppers; Chinese food at a restaurant; local cola and beer. *Cost: $56.76* per week

The Cui family in *Weitaiwu Village, China*, eats rice, cornmeal; small amounts of meat; fruits and vegetables, on which they spend 1/5 of their budget); peanut oil, soy sauce; no prepared or fast food; beer, Coca Cola, tea. *Cost: $57.27* per week

The Dong family in *Beijing, China*, eats rice, white bread; yogurt, Haagan-Dazs ice cream; flatfish, beef, pigs' elbows; peanut oil, soy sauce; some fast food and prepared food; grapefruit juice, Coca Cola, Nescafé coffee. *Cost: $155.06* per week

The Le Moins family in *Montreuil, France*, eats bread, spaghetti, potatoes, croissants, corn flakes; milk, yogurt, cheese; meat and fish, on which they spend 1/4 of their budget; olive oil, jam, mayonnaise; cookies; prepared and fast foods, on which they spend more than 1/4 of their budget; mineral water, juice, wine. *Cost: $419.95* per week

The Melanders family in *Bargteheide, Germany*, eats whole grain bread, potatoes, pasta, croissants; milk, yogurt, ice cream, butter; meat, fish, eggs, on which they spend 1/10 of their budge; fruit and vegetables, on which they spend 1/7 of their budget; olive oil, spices; prepared foods, on which they spend 1/9 of their budget; bottled water, juices, beer, wine. *Cost: $500.07* per week

enough to eat, hundreds of millions more are eating too much and are overweight or obese. Except in the very poorest countries, more people today are overweight than underweight."[4]

In other words, in spite of technological advances, there's still a huge divide in the world between those who have enough—or too much—to eat, and those who aren't sure of their next meal.

EVERY COUNTRY HAS BORROW—OR STOLEN

Tomato-growing began in Italy, right? Otherwise how could pizza have been invented? Not so fast. According to anthropologist Miriam Chaiken, "A lot of what we think of as deeply rooted cultural traditions are really traceable back to global exchange."[5] In other words, from the get-go humans have traded food and ideas about food, so that it's often tricky to determine who ate what first.

A prime example is the tomato we associate with pizza and pasta, which, in fact, came to Europe only after Columbus took back a sample from the New World. Japan got chopsticks from China and tempura from Portugal. In short, every country has borrowed or stolen from the cultures of others.[6]

CODFISH MAKES A ROUND TRIP

The importing and exporting of food, mostly a good thing, sometimes reaches absurdity, for instance, when a codfish caught off Norway is shipped to China for processing and then back to Norway for sale. Or when Argentine lemons are sent to Spain, while Spanish lemons are left to rot on the ground. Or when half of the peas sold in Europe are grown and packaged in Kenya. Or when 15,000 tons of waffles a year are exported from Great Britain and another 15,000 tons are brought in from somewhere else.[7] Transportation is a wonderful thing, except for the pollution it causes, which takes a big toll in money and human health.

OLD TRADITIONS AT RISK

Are you still appreciating the same foods your great grandparents ate? Maybe you and your family are, but Toshihiro Murata is disappointed. Owner of a high-end restaurant in Kyoto, Japan, where the menu includes sea-bream sushi wrapped in bamboo, tiny grilled ayu fish, and fried prawns, he believes that the "Japanese cuisine is something embedded in Japanese people's DNA." Meanwhile his college-age daughter "doesn't see much difference between cheap restaurant food and the haute cuisine he makes."[8]

McDonald's does a big business in Beijing, China.

Not only young people are leaving traditions behind. Changes in eating patterns are affecting everyone. Until recently most Italians ate their main meal (*pranzo*) around 1 P.M., when offices and stores closed and the whole family came home to eat and rest. The first course of pasta, rice, or soup, was ordinarily followed by a small portion of meat and vegetables, and then a finale of fruit. Now, however, with business gone global and worsening traffic, the daily *pranzo* in many Italian families is a thing of the past.

Similar changes can be seen among many people in South America, where migration from country to cities has also upset midday eating habits.

KEEPING TRADITIONS

Not everyone is willing to give up long-standing food traditions. According to writer Bryan Walsh, there's a backlash, or at least a "mini-movement" in some countries "to hold fast to traditional food culture, even as the menu grows ever more international."[9]

There are even few places where McDonald's hasn't established a foothold. In the Middle East, for instance, where extended families live together, instead of working outside, women stay home to prepare food, and religious influences dictate eating habits.

Have you heard the term *slow food*? An international organization hopes you'll jump on their bandwagon. This slow food movement campaigns against fast food and stages events that feature traditional recipes. Other groups, including some in Bolivia, "regularly hold food fairs that celebrate South American staples."[10]

HOW DOES YOUR AGE GROUP FIT INTO THE WORLD PICTURE?

If you're a fast-food consumer, you have plenty of company these days around the globe. A recent Australian study of 3,800 twelve- to fifteen-year-olds showed that "90 percent were consuming unhealthy foods like fast foods, energy-dense snacks and sugar-sweetened drinks on a daily basis. One quarter of respondents admitted eating fast food every day, while more than a third said they hardly ever ate fruit."[11]

The somewhat better news was that one-third reported eating a balanced diet. This study also showed that kids who lived outside of cities ate more vegetables and less fast food than city kids ate, and girls ate more fruit and less fast food and meat than boys ate.[12]

A COMMON THREAD AMONG TEENS

The fries may be thicker in Belgium. Kids in the Netherlands may be used to salted herring and onions as street food. But when it comes to food attitudes and habits, teens throughout the Western world have a lot in common. The HELENA study conducted among 304 teenagers in Europe (from Belgium, Hungary, Spain, Sweden, and the UK), showed that

1. snacking is universal. Most kids ate three meals and snacked after school;

2. most kids considered taste to be the most important factor in food choice, and most claimed to be influenced by parents, especially at breakfast and the evening meal;

3. kids in the survey understood the importance of healthy eating but often found "healthy" food boring, expensive, and inconvenient. Most, even if they knew theories of nutrition, seemed willing to put off worrying about health.[13]

BULGARIANS LIKE CHOCOLATE LESS SWEET

Maybe we're more the same than we are different, but taste preferences still vary among cultures. The Nestle Company, which sells $80 billion worth of food each year, spends over a billion dollars determining slight differences in taste preferences among eaters in the 130 countries where its products are sold.[14] As a result they make 200 different types of Nescafé instant coffee, a wide range of KitKat chocolate bars (Russian KitKats are smaller than Bulgarian, and Bulgarian KitKats aren't as sweet as German). To get it right in all those countries Nestle relies on a staff of 3,700.[15]

THE WAY IT TASTED WHEN YOU WERE A KID

How can we explain these local preferences? According to a Nestle spokesperson, "The taste profile is fixed very early in people's minds." In other words, you like best the food you grew up eating. That's why the company uses as a reference in each country the best homemade example they can find. But even Nestle realizes that being *too* local is costly. Their chocolate-covered vanilla ice cream squares (called Dibs in the United States) have the exact same ice cream inside but, depending on the country, use different chocolate on the outside.[16]

FOOD MISUNDERSTANDINGS

Do you consider your taste to be American? Most Americans today have broad tastes. Many eat more Chinese food and sushi than hot dogs and apple pie. Diversity broadens us, and yet sometimes we—home cooks and even restaurant cooks—don't quite get the food of other cultures right, even when we have good substitute ingredients. Or so says Frank Ferretti, reporter and food writer, in the matter of Chinese food served in the United States.

According to Ferretti, a lover and respecter of Chinese food, "Food is routinely declared Chinese simply because it is marinated in soy sauce." Even though Americans consume Chinese food by the ton, most of what we get isn't authentic, a result of haphazard adaptations from the cooking efforts of male-only Chinese immigrants more than a hundred years ago. We can correct these problems, Ferretti says, and do justice to the Chinese cuisine in the United States, as long as eaters are willing to educate themselves and to challenge chefs.[17]

SENSIBLE SUSPICIONS ABOUT FOOD

Some suspicions about food are sensible. We've already discussed home-food safety in chapter 7 and restaurant safety in chapter 10. Safe eating while traveling in other countries is also important. First, food may be iffy in certain countries because of climactic, governmental, and economic conditions, resulting in careless agricultural practices, poor refrigeration, and inadequate inspection. Second, even if food abroad meets decent standards of health, you may be more vulnerable than usual to various bacteria and chemicals because you're not used to them.

Montezuma's Revenge

Among travelers to foreign countries, "most illnesses come from bacteria, viruses, parasites, and chemicals that contaminate food and water. Some of the more common

"THEY ENDED UP TEACHING ME"

Anelys Fernandez, a student at Bergen Academy in New Jersey and soon-to-be college student, tells about leaving the comfort of home for a summer exchange program.

Throughout my four years of high school I heard many interesting things about a program called Amigos de las Americas, but not once did I imagine myself participating in such a program. This program emphasizes bringing cultures together and teaching others the importance of a balanced diet and the environment. As it turned out, I was chosen to spend six long weeks away from home—away from all that I had ever come to know and love.

I began my first days in Mexico dreading every meal. I had been a vegetarian for 18 months and was in no rush to change. Lunch consisted of mounds of rice with a never-ending supply to tortillas and a small ration of meat, while breakfast and dinner consisted of sweetened bread and watered-down milk. I can't say it was horrible, but what I can say is that it was unhealthy, and it took a major toll on my body.

Every meal was cooked in a pool of pig lard, and vegetables and fruits were nowhere to be seen. Rather than eating the abundant fruits that hung from the trees surrounding their homes, the family let them go bad and fed them to the pigs. Not once did I eat vegetables or a cup of fresh fruit juice. I was constantly visiting the hospital with fevers and aches.

But no matter how badly I felt, I would never have cut my visit short. Being around these hardworking individuals taught me the importance of family and hard work. I was there to teach them what I knew about nutrition and the importance of a balanced diet, but I feel that they ended up teaching me. They taught me that no matter what hardships come your way, you'll always have your family to support you.

When Anelys Fernandez of New Jersey attended a summer exchange program in Mexico, she had to make tough adjustments in her diet.

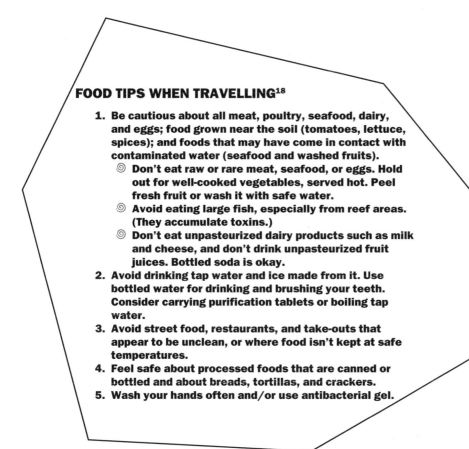

FOOD TIPS WHEN TRAVELLING[18]

1. Be cautious about all meat, poultry, seafood, dairy, and eggs; food grown near the soil (tomatoes, lettuce, spices); and foods that may have come in contact with contaminated water (seafood and washed fruits).
   - Don't eat raw or rare meat, seafood, or eggs. Hold out for well-cooked vegetables, served hot. Peel fresh fruit or wash it with safe water.
   - Avoid eating large fish, especially from reef areas. (They accumulate toxins.)
   - Don't eat unpasteurized dairy products such as milk and cheese, and don't drink unpasteurized fruit juices. Bottled soda is okay.
2. Avoid drinking tap water and ice made from it. Use bottled water for drinking and brushing your teeth. Consider carrying purification tablets or boiling tap water.
3. Avoid street food, restaurants, and take-outs that appear to be unclean, or where food isn't kept at safe temperatures.
4. Feel safe about processed foods that are canned or bottled and about breads, tortillas, and crackers.
5. Wash your hands often and/or use antibacterial gel.

illnesses include traveler's diarrhea, Montezuma's revenge, infectious hepatitis, typhoid fever, cholera, and illness from the *Giardia* parasite."[19]

Montezuma's revenge, if you haven't met the term before, is the version of diarrhea suffered by 40 percent of tourists visiting Mexico.[20] This vacation-ruining health problem was so named as a humorous allusion to Aztec leader Montezuma. Having been defeated in 1519 by the Spaniard Cortes, the Aztec ruler is said to be getting revenge on tourists ever since.

Try not to let the unpleasant subjects of diarrhea, vomiting, headache, and fatigue discourage you from experimenting sensibly with new foods. Staying healthy in other countries is largely a matter of using safe water and following good advice.

Food-Wary U.S. Olympians

In some cases, if you're mistrustful of food abroad, you can take your own with you. Before the 2008 Summer Games in Beijing the United States Olympic Committee made a decision: ship food for its 600 athletes to China, enough to last until they finished competing. This decision was based on fears that steroids, insecticides, additives, and food-borne illnesses common in China would be damaging to American athletes.

To avoid these problems the committee had 25,000 pounds of chicken (plus breakfast cereals, Nutri-Grain bars, and molasses) sent to Beijing two months before the start of the games. Since competitors are prohibited by International Olympic Committee rules from bringing their own food to the Olympic Village, the Americans had to eat in a training center about twenty minutes away.[21]

No surprise—the Beijing government was offended. But they stepped up, nevertheless, to inspect more thoroughly and to insure food safety for the 10,500 participants and 550,000 foreign visitors to the games.[22]

Eating foods of other countries can be fascinating and rewarding. Be cautious and patient—introduce yourself gradually to new foods. Whether you're eating in ethnic restaurants near home or in faraway countries, compare new tastes to those you know borrow ideas if you can.

NOTES

1. Joel Stein, "Extreme Eating," *Time*, January 21, 2008, 68.

2. Peter Menzel and Faith D'Aluisio, *Hungry Planet: What the World Eats* (Napa, CA: Material World Books, 2005), 56–57.

3. Peter Menzel, photographer, and his wife Faith D'Aluisio, writer, collaborated on the book *Hungry Planet*.

4. Marion Nestle, "Dinner for Six Billion," in Menzel and D'Aluisio, *Hungry Planet*, 8.

5. Quoted in Bryan Walsh, "How the World Eats" [electronic version], *Time*, May 30, 2007, 1, www.time.com/time/specials/2007/article/0,28804,1626795_1627112_1626671,00.html (accessed April 22, 2009).

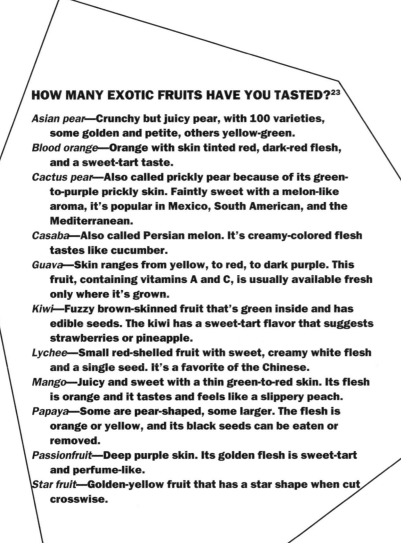

HOW MANY EXOTIC FRUITS HAVE YOU TASTED?[23]

Asian pear—Crunchy but juicy pear, with 100 varieties, some golden and petite, others yellow-green.

Blood orange—Orange with skin tinted red, dark-red flesh, and a sweet-tart taste.

Cactus pear—Also called prickly pear because of its green-to-purple prickly skin. Faintly sweet with a melon-like aroma, it's popular in Mexico, South American, and the Mediterranean.

Casaba—Also called Persian melon. It's creamy-colored flesh tastes like cucumber.

Guava—Skin ranges from yellow, to red, to dark purple. This fruit, containing vitamins A and C, is usually available fresh only where it's grown.

Kiwi—Fuzzy brown-skinned fruit that's green inside and has edible seeds. The kiwi has a sweet-tart flavor that suggests strawberries or pineapple.

Lychee—Small red-shelled fruit with sweet, creamy white flesh and a single seed. It's a favorite of the Chinese.

Mango—Juicy and sweet with a thin green-to-red skin. Its flesh is orange and it tastes and feels like a slippery peach.

Papaya—Some are pear-shaped, some larger. The flesh is orange or yellow, and its black seeds can be eaten or removed.

Passionfruit—Deep purple skin. Its golden flesh is sweet-tart and perfume-like.

Star fruit—Golden-yellow fruit that has a star shape when cut crosswise.

6. Walsh, "How the World Eats," 1.

7. Elisabeth Rosenthal, "Environmental Cost of Shipping Groceries around the World," *New York Times*, April 26, 2008, www.nytimes.com/2008/04/26/business/worldbusiness/26food.html (accessed November 20, 2008).

8. Walsh, "How the World Eats," 1.

9. Walsh, "How the World Eats," 2.

10. Bryan Walsh, "How the World Eats" [print version], *Time*, June 11, 2007, 80.

11. "Teens' Fast Food Addiction," *Herald Sun*, April 11, 2007, www.news.com.au/heraldsun/story/0,21985,21538877–24331,00. html (accessed May 8, 2008).

12. "Teens' Fast Food Addiction."

13. "Finding Out More about Food Choices and Preferences of Adolescents in Europe," EUFIC, www.eufic.org/article/en/health-and-lifestyle/food-for-all-ages/artid/food-choices-preferences-adolescents-Europe/ (accessed January 6, 2008).

14. Peter Gumbel, "Taste Test: Same but Different," *Time*, June 13, 2007, 1, www.time.com/time/specials/2007/article/0,28804,1628191_1626317_1632275,00.html (accessed April 22, 2009).

15. Gumbel, "Taste Test," 2.

16. Gumbel, "Taste Test," 4–5.

17. Fred Ferretti, "A Rat in the Kitchen," *New York Times,* February 9, 2008, A15.

18. Richard H. Linton, "Food Safety Advice When Traveling Abroad," Purdue University Food Safety Issues, FS-11, December 1999, www.ces.purdue.edu/extmedia/FS/FS-11/FS-11.html (accessed April 30, 2009).

19. Linton, "Food Safety Advice When Travelling Abroad."

20. "Montezuma's Revenge," *Wikipedia*, en.wikipedia.org/wiki/Montezuma%27s_Revenge_%28illness%29#Montezuma.27s_Revenge (accessed May 1, 2009).

21. Ben Shpigel, "Wary of Food, U.S. Olympians Plan a Big Delivery to China," *New York Times*, February 9, 2008, A1, A6.

22. "Beijing Says Food Safe for Olympic Athletes, Tourists," Bio-Medicine, www.bio-medicine.org/medicine-news/Beijing-Says-Food-Safe-for-Olympic-Athletes--Tourists-23932-1/ (accessed May 1, 2009).

23. "Exploring Exotic Fruits," SHEKNOWS, www.sheknows.com/articles/7164.htm (accessed November 28, 2009).

13 The Future of Food

How do you picture yourself in connection with food in the future? Sarah, age sixteen, says, "I will own my own restaurant and bakery. I will be the first truly world famous vegetarian chef. Not only will I prove the virtues of tofu to the narrow-minded steak eaters of the world, I will also, eventually, master making a pie crust. Not only will I earn five stars from Zagat, I will convince my mother to try Indian food. I will enrich my own life and lives of others through food, trying to make the world a better place along the way."

Maybe you won't go to food markets. You'll order food online and have it sent to where you live. Before taking exams, your kids will eat brain-enhancing and anti-tiredness foods. For convenience you'll buy square apples for easy packing. No need to wait, though for those innovations. They already exist. The future is now.

PREDICTIONS

It's fun to predict long-range outcomes, and we keep trying, no matter how useless. Think about past goofs, such as "We'll get all our nutrition in pill form," or "Who will be willing to watch ads on television?" What do *you* think the food future holds, for yourself and for the world? Humorist Woody Allen says, "I have seen the future, and it's very much like the present, only longer."

NUMBER 1 QUESTION: WILL WE RUN OUT OF FOOD?

A lot of experts believe we have reason to worry about starvation in the future. If you just ate lunch and have a full refrigerator at home, you're probably not one of the worriers. When it comes to dealing with huge global problems, most of us are good at postponing. Not David Leavitt.

After visiting a homeless shelter when he was a young teenager, David began a mission to help the hungry. What started as a bar mitzvah project developed into a program in Seminole, Florida, involving ninety-two schools. With the support of his mother, David influenced his school board and various business people, so that "in one school year alone, 55,000 pounds of school food were donated to the hungry." Kids at his middle school called him "charity boy," but that didn't bother him much back then, and now, he says, his friends think what he's doing is cool.[1]

What's the Story on World Hunger

How big is the problem of hunger? How does it show itself? And what's being done? Before looking at the answers, take a guess.

1. **Who predicted, back in 1798, that population would grow faster than our ability to produce food?**
   a. **Benjamin Franklin**
   b. **T. R. Malthus**
   c. **King George of England**

Answer: The English political economist and pastor named Malthus. The term *Malthusian* is still used to refer to this view that mankind was doomed to starvation. As it turned out, birth control and agricultural technology have saved us, so far.

2. **About how many people in the world today can be said to be starving?**

a. 8 million

b. 80 million

c. 800 million

Answer: If you guessed c, you're right.

3. **Where in the world are the greatest numbers of hungry people?**

a. India

b. China

c. Sub-Saharan and North Africa

Answer: In all of the above. Hunger is also rampant in the Near East, Latin America, and the Caribbean.

4. **What percentage of hungry people are living in cities?**

a. 10 percent

b. 20 percent

c. 50 percent

Answer: Twenty percent. Fifty percent of the hungry are small farmers and the rest are mostly landless country people.[2]

5. **Of those people who are hungry, what percentage are women?**

a. 30 percent

b. 50 percent

c. 60 percent

Answer: Sixty percent of the hungry are women and girls, even though throughout much of the world they're the main ones working the soil.[3]

6. **In the same places where people are starving, we often find**

a. poor soil and bad weather

b. civil war and poor governing

c. AIDS epidemics

Answer: Again, all of the above. Hunger also goes hand-in-hand with unfair distribution of money and backward technology and education.

7. **World Bank president Robert Zoellick warned, in 2008, that rising food prices were putting thirty-three nations at risk. Within the following year, how many countries actually experienced food riots?**

   a. **10**

   b. **20**

   c. **30**

Answer: Thirty. In other words, *in our own time*, people are fighting over food.[4]

8. **Food shortages are often the result of factors we can't control, like floods and droughts. What is a main threat to food production that we *can* do something about?**

   a. **Decreasing number of working farms**

   b. **Growing numbers of illegal immigrants**

   c. **Increasing demand for meat**

Answer: If you guessed c, you're right. A big part of the world's food predicament can be traced to the fact that people who always ate meat are eating more of it, and many who couldn't afford it in the past are trying to catch up. A continuing demand for meat may cause fossil fuels to run out and will surely result in scarcity and contamination of food and water.[5]

9. **Which organization is most involved in trying to alleviate world hunger?**

   a. **U.S. Department of Agriculture**

   b. **United Nations World Food Program**

   c. **Red Cross**

Answer: The United Nations' World Food Program, headquartered in Rome, is the world's largest humanitarian agency. In 2008 they established a special emergency Hunger Task Force. Charitable organizations such as the Red Cross and Concern Worldwide are collaborating on this initiative.[6]

Many other groups—private, religious, and governmental—contribute money, manpower, and expertise in the effort to end starvation. Two well-known hunger-relief organizations are Oxfam and Heifer International.

10. So what's the bottom line—will we run out of food?

   a. Yes

   b. No

   c. Maybe

Answer: Depends on whom you ask. Optimists at the Bread for the World Institute believe we could feed the world's poor for less money than Americans and Europeans spend on pet food each year.[7] Meanwhile writer-economist Paul Roberts is one of many who think we're "closer to the precipice than we have ever been, yet perhaps more capable, ultimately, of stepping away."[8]

NEXT QUESTION FOR THE FUTURE: CAN WE STOP EATING TOO MUCH?

"Too much food can be nearly as big a problem as too little."

—Michael Pollan, "Famer in Chief"[9]

Can you see yourself maintaining your ideal weight as you reach the age of your parents? If so, you may be able to head off heart disease, diabetes, and cancer. And if you keep weight down, you'll be helping not only yourself but society. Everyone who overeats contributes incrementally to extra greenhouse gases in the atmosphere, which results in pollution of air and water and leads to global warming.[10]

What Can Governments Do to Help?

This country could take action against overfeeding by rethinking farm subsidies. Instead of continuing to protect

---

CAN WE SLOW DOWN THE MEATEATERS?

1. In the last 50 years, the world's total meat consumption has grown four times greater.[11] Many who once couldn't afford meat now can afford it, and they want to catch up to the rest of us.
2. Much grain that could feed hungry people is now fed to animals. If four people are starving, should a pound of grain be divided among them, or go to one animal being raised for meat?
3. Demand for meat affects us all, even vegetarians. Providing grain for both humas and animals strains and pollutes the environment. For instance, in June of 1995, a lagoon of hog waste "burst into a river in North Carolina, destroying aquatic life for 17 miles.[12]

---

corn, the government could offer subsidies to farmers dedicated to organic produce, diversity of crops, and the raising of grass-fed animals in an economy that relies on soil, water, and sunlight rather than massive machinery and chemicals.

Japan Is Measuring Waists

How would you feel about being required to have your waist measured once a year? The Japanese aren't known for being overfed, but they want to keep it that way. Under a national law established in 2008, companies and local governments must measure the waistlines of people between the ages of 40 and 74 as part of their annual checkups. Any of the 56 million people measured who go over the government limit (33.5 inches for men and 35.4 for women) have to submit to diet education. Companies and local governments that fail to meet weight-loss targets within four years will have to pay financial penalties.[13]

In the Netherlands They're Researching Eating Habits

If you don't like being watched while you eat, you wouldn't be volunteering at the Restaurant of the Future. Luckily for economist-director Rene Koster, the 250 students and staff members involved in this ten-year study in Holland don't mind having every bite recorded by two dozen hidden cameras. And they don't mind being weighed by invisible floor scales, or having their heart rates measured automatically by the chairs they're sitting in.

What's the point? To discover what makes people eat and drink the way they do, in order to provide useful information to policy makers and health experts. Why would anyone participate? "Because this research is a good idea and the food is better than in the other canteens," says Bert Meurs, plant scientist and volunteer. One short-term benefit is salvaging food waste for compost (one-third of all served food in the Netherlands would otherwise be tossed out).[14]

What's being done in the U.S.?

NEXT QUESTION: WILL FOOD BE LESS SAFE IN THE FUTURE?

Paul Roberts, food economist, admits he's more likely to die in a car crash than from food poisoning, but he's still concerned about the fact that certain pathogens like Listeria and salmonella have become more prevalent and more resistant to antibiotics.[15] "More resistant" is a calm way of saying that those bad bugs are getting impossible to kill. The good news is we're more adept now at detecting food-safety problems. The bad news is, because of global food exchanges, "pathogens can now move between countries and regions with greater ease."[16]

More good-news/bad-news. On the one hand the USDA (U.S. Department of Agriculture) has initiated HACCP—Hazard Analysis and Critical Control Point—which means that foods are inspected earlier in production, in order to detect problems sooner. On the other hand, HACCP inspection and other USDA protocols cover only American-produced foods—not the one-eighth of all we eat that is imported from other countries.[17]

Fish of the Future—and Now

Speaking of imported, have you eaten fish lately—maybe a fish sandwich? Fish in markets, these days, are usually labeled by country of origin, but in restaurants and fast-food outlets, who knows where they're from? The chances are pretty good that your fish sandwich is a cheaply produced catfish-like thing, known as pangius, or tra, being "farmed" in Vietnam or some other Asian country. The farm is a pond, "almost more fish than water," where "two-foot-long creatures, gray on top, white on bottom, with faces resembling a slightly dimwitted 'Star Wars' character, interlock and wriggle."[18]

Funny-looking, however, isn't the problem. And the fact that these fish are coming from Asia isn't the problem. The problem is, what have those wrigglers been fed in that pond? Even if they aren't literally being raised in latrine ponds today, as they once were, these fish have been treated with cancer-causing fungicides and antibiotics banned in the United States.[19] "Farm-raised" fish may sound purer than wild fish, but don't kid yourself.

Even though self-described "wild-fish snob" food writer Mark Bittman admits that not all fish farming is bad, he urges you to bypass farmed fish and develop a taste for so-called forage fish, such as herring, mackerel, anchovies, and sardines, which are more nutritious and less expensive.[20]

Fish in the future are likely to be scarcer. Global consumption has doubled in the last thirty-five years. Catching fish is harder and more expensive than farm-raising them. A recent study predicts that if current fishing practices continue "the world's major commercial stocks will collapse by 2048."[21] Eat wild fish while you can.

WHAT ELSE DOES THE FUTURE HOLD?

Tastier produce and meats, if Joel Salatin gets his way. If you're rooting for organic, local, solar food in the future,

Reliable fish markets indicate where each fish comes from. "Farm fresh" may sound healthy, but wild, local, fresh, and natural are preferable.

you'll find a model on his Polyface Farm in Virginia, where Salatin raises chicken, beef, turkeys, eggs, rabbits, and pigs; various vegetables; and berries on "one hundred acres of pasture patchworked into another 450 acres of forest." Salatin thinks of himself as a grass farmer, because grasses are the "foundation of the intricate food chain."[22]

Anchovy-Laced Orange Juice?

Let's say, even though you know they're good for you, you can't stand the taste of sardines, broccoli, or pomegranate juice. Suppose anchovies and sardines, rich in nutritious omega-3 fatty acids, could be ground up, deodorized, and added to orange juice, which you like? The result wouldn't be artificial because the additives would be natural. And the additives wouldn't be in pill form. They would be hidden but present—minus their odor—in foods you like. According to *New York Times* writer

Julia Moskin, these so-called nutraceutical-added foods already exist or are in the works.[23]

Revolutionary Apples

Are you ready for square apples? Although the Japanese got a head start by developing a square watermelon in the 1980s, more recently Lee Chong Boun, a Korean Nike-shop-owner-turned-farmer, has got a reshaped apple for you. Helped by his local government, after five years' work he was able to grow "cubic apples" in plastic containers that are attached to branches of apple trees. At this point, at seven dollars each, the market appears to be limited, but maybe some people will be willing to pay for easy-fit-in-the-frig or for sheer novelty.[24] Super rice, square fruit, and low-cal potatoes are some of today's novel ideas that may end up as food staples of the future.

WHAT CAN *YOU* DO FOR THE FUTURE OF FOOD?

1. *Eat less meat.* Instead of the 190 pounds a year, on average, that each American consumes (a half pound a day),[25] try adding a little meat to a stir-fry and saving the planet.
2. *Waste less food.* "The USDA estimates that Americans throw out 14 percent of the food they buy."[26] And if you have to throw something out, turn it into compost.
3. *Raise food yourself, if possible, and eat local food.*
4. *"Vote" against processed foods and their marketers by refusing to buy junk.*
5. *Keep your ears and mind alert for food information in school and the media.*

SO WHAT ELSE IS NEW?

Genetically modified (GM) food. If square apples and low-cholesterol chickens are the norm in the future, we'll have gotten them through genetic modification (engineering). Because the idea of fooling around with genes makes a lot of people nervous, developments in this area will probably be gradual. Of course we've been genetically modifying food and animals for centuries through the more natural process of selective breeding.

Selective breeding means, for instance, taking seeds from plants that showed resistance to fungus and planting those seeds exclusively, to get fungus-resistant plants. Animals can also be bred to enhance certain desirable characteristics as most people know from observing show dogs and race horses.

Genetic modification however, isn't a farming method. In selective breeding, the transfer of genes is only between closely related species, but in genetic engineering, "genes from the same species or from *any* other species, even those from animals, can be introduced into plants."[27]

What Do We Gain by Modifying Food?

Already in use is the herbicide Roundup, which eliminates weeds but not crops. This herbicide targets weeds and but leaves unharmed soybeans and other plants that have been genetically modified to resist it.[28]

Other developments on the horizon are bananas modified to protect people against hepatitis B, fish and fruit and nut trees that mature faster, and cows resistant to mad cow disease.[29]

Controversy over GM Foods

In 2006, GM crops were planted in twenty-two countries, led by the United States, with 53 percent of the total. The main modified crops were soybeans, corn, cotton, canola, and alfalfa, all resistant to herbicides. Other experiments have produced sweet potatoes resistant to a particular virus, rice with increased iron and vitamins, and plants able to survive weather extremes.[30]

The idea of tampering with nature scares some people. On the one hand, GM foods may help us meet some of the greatest challenges of the future. On the other hand, we can't ignore potential risks, known and unknown. Controversy focuses on human health and environmental safety, labeling, and ethics. Potential problems are (1) long-range health problems for eaters, associated with allergens and antibiotic resistance markers; (2) negative effects on the environment; (3) confusion in the labeling of GM and non-GM products; (4) religious or philosophical objections to altering nature; and (5) monopolies on the part of rich countries.[31]

Some experts are optimistic about solving genetic-engineering problems. Authors and researchers Pamela Ronald and Raoul Adamchak—a married couple—believe that GM and organic foods can be joined in a way that will satisfy the needs of the predicted world population in 2050—9.2 billion, up from 6.7 billion now.[32]

When the author of *Future Files*, Paul Watson, looks into his crystal ball, he sees lots of polar opposites when it comes to food habits. Some of us are eating locally, some globally. Some are eating healthily, some indulgently. Some of us are trying the latest thing, some are traditional. Low cost and luxurious. Fast and slow: "For most people," he says, "convenience will be everything. . . . Sometimes what people eat will be healthy but for the most part it will be comfort food. . . . We will see people swinging from indulgence to health on a daily or weekly basis."[33]

In other words, futurist Watson's predictions sound something like Woody Allen's—namely, the future in food will be "very much like the present, only longer."

NOTES

1. Susan Perry, *Catch the Spirit* (New York: Franklin Watts, 2000), 15–19.

2. Paul Roberts, *The End of Food* (New York: Houghton Mifflin, 2008), 322.

218

3. "What the *New York Times* Couldn't Swallow," Raj's Blog, stuffedandstarved.org/drupal/node/420 (accessed January 24, 2009).

4. Michael Pollan, "Farmer in Chief," *New York Times Magazine*, October 12, 2008, 64.

5. Mark Bittman, "Rethinking the Meat Guzzler," *New York Times*, January 27, 2008, wk, 1, and Bee Wilson, "The Last Bite," *New Yorker*, May 19, 2008, 76.

6. Sharman Apt Russell, *Hunger: An Unnatural History* (New York: Basic Books, 2005), 207–8.

7. "Hunger Facts," Bread for the World, www.bread.org/learn/hunger-basics/ (accessed May 12, 2009).

8. Roberts, *The End of Food*, 322.

9. Pollan, "Farmer in Chief," 64.

10. Pollan, "Farmer in Chief," 64.

11. Mark Bittman, "Rethinking the Meat Guzzler," *New York Times*, January 27, 2008, WK, 1.

12. Paul Roberts, in *The End of Food*, quoted in Bee Wilson's "The Last Bite," *New Yorker*, May 19, 2008.

13. Norimitsu Onishi, "Japan, Seeking Trim Waists, Decides to Measure Millions," *New York Times*, international edition, June 13, 2008, A1.

14. Marlise Simons, "In the Netherlands, Eat, Drink and Be Monitored," *New York Times*, international edition, November 26, 2007, A2.

15. Roberts, *The End of Food*, 177.

16. Roberts, *The End of Food*, 178.

17. Roberts, *The End of Food*, 182–84.

18. Paul Greenberg, "A Catfish by Any Other Name," *New York Times Magazine*, October 12, 2008, 74–75.[AU]

19. Greenberg, "A Catfish by Any Other Name," 74–75.

20. Mark Bittman, "A Seafood Snob Ponders the Future of Fish," *New York Times*, November 16, 2008, 4.

21. Bittman, "A Seafood Snob Ponders the Future of Fish," 4.

22. Michael Pollan, *The Omnivore's Dilemma* (New York: Penguin Books, 2006), 125–27, 203.

23. Julia Moskin, "Superfood or Monster from the Deep?" *New York Times*, September 17, 2008, F1.

24. Jennifer Veale, "Revolution in the Garden," *Time*, June 2007, no page number.

25. Pollan, "Farmer in Chief," 64.

26. Pollan, "Farmer in Chief," 66.

27. Pamela C. Ronald and Raoul W. Adamchak, *Tomorrow's Table* (New York: Oxford University Press, 2008), x.

28. Ronald and Adamchak, *Tomorrow's Table*, x.

29. "What Are Genetically Modified (GM) Foods?" Human Genome Project Information, 1–2, www.ornl.gov/sci/techresources/Human_Genome/elsi/gmfood.shtml (accessed May 12, 2009).

30. "What Are Genetically Modified (GM) Foods?" 1–2.

31. "What Are Genetically Modified (GM) Foods?" 2–3.

32. Ronald and Adamchak, *Tomorrow's Table*, x.

33. Richard Watson, *Future Files* (London: Nicholas Brearley Publishing, 2008), 179.

Index

About the Author

Robin F. Brancato was born in Reading, Pennsylvania, graduated from the University of Pennsylvania and the City University of New York, and has spent her adult life writing and teaching. She is the mother of two sons and the author of eight young adult novels, including the ALA Notable Book *Winning*. Her previous contribution to the It Happened to Me series was *Money: Getting It, Using It, and Avoiding the Traps*. She currently lives in Fort Lee, New Jersey.